LIMITED EDITION

Designed and Bound by National Publishing Co.
Original Version Published by Creative Homeowner
Text Printed by Courier Kendallville
Cover Printed by Moore Langen
Limited Edition Page Printed by Courier Stoughton
Logistics by Courier Fulfillment Services
Courier 2009

EVERYBODY GRILLS!®

EVERYBODY GRILLS!®

200 Prize-Worthy Recipes to Put SIZZLE ON YOUR GRILL

CREATIVE HOMEOWNER®, Upper Saddle River, New Jersey

COPYRIGHT © 2008

CRE**A**TIVE
HOMEOWNER®

A Division of Federal Marketing Corp.
Upper Saddle River, NJ

CHAR-BROIL EVERYBODY GRILLS®!

EDITOR Lisa Kahn
PRINCIPAL PHOTOGRAPHER Glenn Moores
FOOD STYLIST Trudy Hewer
GRILL CHEF Stuart Marston
PHOTOGRAPHIC COORDINATOR Contact Jupiter Inc.
DESIGN AND LAYOUT David Geer
JUNIOR EDITOR Jennifer Calvert
EDITORIAL ASSISTANT Nora Grace
DIGITAL IMAGE COORDINATOR Robyn Poplasky
DIGITAL IMAGING SPECIALIST Frank Dyer
INDEXER Schroeder Indexing Services

CREATIVE HOMEOWNER

VICE PRESIDENT AND PUBLISHER Timothy O. Bakke
PRODUCTION DIRECTOR Kimberly H. Vivas
ART DIRECTOR David Geer
MANAGING EDITOR Fran J. Donegan

Current Printing (last digit)
10 9 8 7 6 5

Manufactured in the United States of America

Char-Broil Everybody Grills®!, First Edition
Library of Congress Control Number: 2007942992
ISBN-10: 1-58011-208-0
ISBN-13: 978-1-58011-208-6

CREATIVE HOMEOWNER®
A Division of Federal Marketing Corp.
24 Park Way
Upper Saddle River, NJ 07458
www.creativehomeowner.com

ALL PHOTOGRAPHY BY GLENN MOORES EXCEPT WHERE NOTED.

page 9: *bottom right* Bill Shanks; **page 13:** *bottom* courtesy Char-Broil; **page 14:** *top* courtesy Char-Broil; **page 15:** courtesy Char-Broil; **page 16:** courtesy Char-Broil; **page 17:** courtesy Char-Broil; **page 19:** courtesy Char-Broil

Planet Friendly Publishing
GREEN EDITION
✓ Made in the United States
✓ Printed on Recycled Paper
Text: 10%   Cover: 10%
Learn more: www.greenedition.org

At Creative Homeowner we're committed to producing books in an earth-friendly manner and to helping our customers make greener choices.

Manufacturing books in the United States ensures compliance with strict environmental laws and eliminates the need for international freight shipping, a major contributor to global air pollution.

And printing on recycled paper helps minimize our consumption of trees, water, and fossil fuels. *Char-Broil Everybody Grills!* was printed on paper made with 10% post-consumer waste. According to Environmental Defense's Paper Calculator, by using this innovative paper instead of conventional papers, we achieved the following environmental benefits:

Trees Saved: 56

Water Saved: 20,235 gallons

Solid Waste Eliminated: 3,348 pounds

Air Emissions Eliminated: 6,173 pounds

For more information on our environmental practices, please visit us online at www.creativehomeowner.com/green

ACKNOWLEDGMENTS

This book is dedicated to everyone who has ever waited in line for a grilled hot dog, hamburger, steak, or chicken leg at a family reunion, ball game, church social, company picnic, or the neighbors' backyard, and thought "I can do this better!" At Char-Broil, our goal for building each grill, smoker, and cooking tool is to help you enjoy cooking outdoors for your family and friends. We hope you try the recipes we've gathered here, and that you adapt each one to suit your tastes. C'mon along and join us, because we won't be satisfied until we can say *Everybody Grills!*

CONTENTS

INTRODUCTION

It's my pleasure and honor to welcome you to this very special compilation of great backyard grilling recipes. My involvement with this book is a natural extension of a job I love: creating new recipes and techniques and writing about them for *Sizzle on the Grill,* a newsletter and Web log sponsored by the folks at Char-Broil.

One of the best parts of my work is getting "invited" to thousands of backyard barbecues through the stories and recipes folks pass on to me. It's as if we're all sitting at one big table, enjoying each other's company as we reach for seconds. And now, through *Everybody Grills!,* I'm inviting you to share a place at that table.

I expect that there are many people who are better cooks than I—and you may be one of them. The goal of this book is simply to inspire you to prepare food on your grill that pleases your palate and is adapted to your skills and taste. You'll find a wide range of ingredients and cooking techniques for everything from appetizers to desserts on these pages, all with simple-to-follow instructions. Some recipes, such as "Champion BBQ Beef Brisket," page 86; "Kansas City Mop Ribs," page 104; and "Judge Steve's World-Famous Recipe for Smoking Turkey," page 176, are BBQ-contest classics

adapted for your backyard enjoyment. Others, such as "Smoked Pecans and Gouda," page 27; "Indian-Spice Grilled Cauliflower," page 238; and "Adam Byrd's Grilled Blackberry Cobbler," page 258, will challenge you to experiment by grilling new types of foods—with delicious results. Happy Grilling!

CB

BARRY "CB" MARTIN

1 Everybody Outside!

The material in this chapter was contributed by Barry "CB" Martin, author of "Sizzle on the Grill," the weekly newsletter and Web log sponsored by Char-Broil, LLC.

IT'S ALL ABOUT THE HEAT

The roots of modern grilling go back to prehistoric times when our ancestors placed a chunk of meat on a stick and held it in the fire. Judging by the number of people who love outdoor cooking today, there's something in the way the intense heat crisps the meat's surface that still appeals to our deeply rooted DNA.

While we've refined the caveman's cooking tools and techniques a bit over the ensuing eons, there are certain things that haven't changed. The most important of these is the management of heat. This is probably the most basic skill required of any good cook, whether they're preparing a meal in the kitchen or the backyard. But because this book is about outdoor cooking, let's start with some basic facts about the heat we use to grill, barbecue, and smoke food.

In outdoor cooking, the heat source we use most often is fire. Whether its source is the propane in a gas grill, the charcoal in a smoker, or the logs on a campfire, fire produces heat; and we can harness that heat to cook foods to our delight.

Fire requires three things to burn: combustible material, a supply of oxygen, and a source of ignition. There are many materials that can burn; yet only a few—such as wood, charcoal, and propane or natural gas—are suitable for cooking food.

Outdoor cooking enthusiasts often refer to heat as either **direct** or **indirect**. The most popular form of **direct-heat** cooking is **grilling,** which means cooking food directly over the heat source, usually at high temperatures. We typically grill steaks, chops, burgers, and fish. We can also use a grill's **indirect heat** to cook food more slowly and at lower temperatures further away from the heat source. Whole chickens, briskets, roasts, and other large cuts of meat are usually cooked by this method, which we generally call **barbecuing.**

INFRARED HEAT generated by a well-prepared charcoal fire.

GRILLING, BARBECUING & SMOKING: WHAT'S THE DIFFERENCE?

Many people mistakenly refer to any type of cooking on their grill as "barbecuing," but that's not entirely correct. Let's compare the outdoor cooking techniques needed for the recipes in this book.

Grilling

Grilling involves quickly cooking individual portions of food at relatively high temperatures over a direct heat source. The first step in many grilling recipes is to **sear** the meat over high heat—between 350°F to 550°F. The higher heat browns the outside of smaller cuts of meat, sealing in juices that would be lost if the meat were cooked more slowly. My mother did this before placing a roast in the oven, and I do it every time I grill a steak. Cast-iron grates on a grill are also highly conductive, which significantly aids the searing process.

Once food is seared, you'll often finish cooking over indirect heat on another part of the grill. The reason food can continue to cook this way is that there's still plenty of heat generated by one or more of these sources: 1) **convective** heat from air heated by the fire; 2) **conductive** heat from the grill grates; and 3) **radiant** heat produced by either a charcoal or an infrared gas grill.

GRILLING is a quick way to both sear and add a smoky flavor to vegetables, steaks, and chicken.

Grilled Ham with Lemon-Orange Glaze, page 138

BARBECUING "low and slow" works best for large, less-tender cuts of meat, such as pork shoulder.

Barbecuing

Barbecuing is a slower way of cooking large portions of meat or poultry using an **indirect** source of heat at a lower temperature (usually between 225°F to 350°F). It takes time, but your end result is tender and juicy.

Here's the science behind barbecue: when meat is placed away from the heat source, it cooks by "bathing" in the hot air—or convective heat—generated by the fire. Another way you might describe barbecuing is slow roasting at low temperatures. Cuts of meat that benefit from this type of cooking, such as pork shoulder and beef brisket, have a high ratio of collagen in the meat. (Translation: they're tough.) Slow cooking with indirect heat works magic on these cuts, breaking down the dense collagen and adding tenderness and flavor.

Talk to any long-time outdoor cooking enthusiast and sooner or later you're going to hear the phrase "low and slow." In fact, it's pretty much the official motto of all barbecue. "Low" refers to temperature—generally between 225°F to 350°F. "Slow" means the time it takes to cook the food. Simply stated, "Good eating comes to those who cook low and slow."

Smoking

Smoking is the process of cooking food on or near an open fire made from materials such as wood or charcoal. The fire releases particles of these materials into the smoker that impart a unique flavor to the meat. The more these materials smolder and generate smoke, the greater the number of particles to flavor the food. Cooking at temperatures between 140°F–225°F is called **hot smoking.**

If the smoke passes through a cooling chamber and comes into contact with the food at a temperature of around 45°F, you are **cold smoking** the food. (Note: cold-smoked food isn't actually cooked, it's simply being slow-cured and flavored.)

When moisture is added to the smoker to increase its humidity level, it is called **wet smoking.** A simple pan of water is placed away from direct heat inside the grill or smoker. If desired, you can use fruit juice or wine instead of water, or add these liquids to the water for an additional flavor boost.

SMOKING with wood or charcoal on a charcoal grill such as Char-Broil's CB940 (right) uses indirect heat.

Rotisserie-Roasted Leg of Lamb, page 92

ROTISSERIE cooking is ideal for evenly cooking large roasts, whole poultry, lamb, and pork.

Rotisserie Cooking

Rotisserie cooking involves skewering a large piece of meat or poultry on a rotating spit set over your grill's heat source. The spit, usually driven by an electric or battery-powered motor, turns at a constant speed to allow for even cooking over the entire surface of the food. Rotisserie cooking is best for large roasts, whole poultry, and pork.

To check for doneness with rotisserie-grilled food, stop the rotisserie motor and insert an instant-read meat thermometer into the deepest part of the food. To avoid overcooking the food, check the temperature about 15 to 20 minutes before the final estimated cooking time. Always use heat-resistant gloves when removing the rotisserie spit rod from the grill because it can get very hot.

INFRARED COOKING:
WHAT IS IT & HOW DOES IT WORK?

Infrared is a natural form of radiant heat we've all experienced in our daily lives. The warm rays of the sun are transferred to your skin by infrared heat waves. And if you've ever made "sun tea," you've brewed it using the sun's infrared heat.

Charcoal has been used to cook food for centuries and is still prized by some folks today for the flavor it imparts to food. But I bet that many don't realize that it's the infrared heat produced by a charcoal fire that helps food retain its juiciness and flavor. However, charcoal fires require a little more time and effort to adequately prepare them for grilling.

With the introduction of an affordable line of gas grills equipped with infrared, Char-Broil has made the technology used for decades by professional chefs available to backyard grillers. You'll find this exciting technology in Char-Broil's Quantum and RED grills, as well as The Big Easy, Char-Broil's new infrared turkey fryer that cooks without using a drop of oil.

How It Works

Infrared heat is a great way to cook because it can generate high temperatures for quicker cooking and searing—up to two times greater than traditional grills. The infrared waves start to cook the food the instant they reach its surface, quickly creating a sear on the meat that locks in moisture and creates exceptional browning. Char-Broil's infrared cooking systems offer a wide temperature range, from high-heat searing to "slow and low" barbecuing and rotisserie grilling. Because most flare-ups are eliminated, you can simply drop unsoaked wood chips between the grill grates to create a slow-cooked smokehouse flavor in a fraction of the time, using one-third less fuel than standard convection gas grills.

Infrared Cooking Tips

Experience with your new infrared grill will help you determine what temperatures and cooking times deliver the best results. At first, you may want to adjust your regular cooking times. If you have cooked on a charcoal fire, this should be fairly easy to do. If you are more familiar with cooking on a regular convection gas grill, reduce the heat settings you normally use by at least 30 percent, and the cooking time by about 50 percent. Here are some other ideas that will help you master infrared cooking:

- Coat each piece of meat, fish, or poultry with a light spray of high-heat oil, such as canola.
- Plan your cooking according to technique, required times, and the best use of the grill surface. For example, steaks can be seared over high heat then finished over medium or low heat. Begin with steaks you intend to cook to medium doneness, and end with those you want rare.

No-Oil "Deep Frying"

Deep-fried turkey is the juiciest, tastiest, most crisp-skinned bird you'll ever eat. The Big Easy is an oil-less way to "fry" a turkey using infrared technology. Turkeys cooked in The Big Easy are prepped the same way as for traditional fryers. One of the many bonuses of The Big Easy, however, is that you can use dry rubs and seasonings on the outside of the bird.

THE BIG EASY is a safe, easy, and delicious way to cook fried turkey, rotisserie-style chicken, BBQ pork, roast beef—even vegetables.

CARING FOR YOUR GRILL

Like most people, I'm more motivated to clean up after I finish cooking when the weather's nice. But when it's cold and dark outside, I'd rather run back into the house—balancing a plate of hot food while I dodge the raindrops—than clean the grill.

Excuses. Excuses. I'm just lazy sometimes. Here are a few tips and tricks I've learned over the years. Of course, be sure to check the manufacturer's directions for your grill before trying any of these.

Why Clean?

If it's been a while since you last cleaned your cooking grates, here's a tip that could save you time and actually get your grates a lot cleaner. Place either a half-sheet aluminum pan or double layers of heavy-duty aluminum foil on the grates; close the lid; and turn the heat to the highest setting. (This method traps heat, causing the grill temperature to rise to between 500°F–600°F). Let the grates "cook" for about 25–30 minutes. The crud should mostly burn off and, with a light scrape from your grill brush, it all goes into the trash. Beautiful!

Grill Racks and Grates

Before and after each use, you should burn off any excess grease and food that has accumulated on your grates. Turn the grill to high, and close the lid. Leave it on for around 15 minutes; this should turn most debris to ash. When grates have cooled, scrub with a cleaning brush or pad, and they should be as good as new.

Stainless-Steel Grates. Stainless-steel grates should be cleaned regularly with a heavy-duty grill brush. You can occasionally soak the grates in a mixture of water and vinegar. Periodically, remove the grates, and brush them off or lightly bang them together to remove burnt-on debris. Apply vegetable oil after cleaning to help prevent rusting.

Cast-Iron Grates. Treat your cast-iron grates the way you would a favorite cast-iron pan. To prevent rusting, cast iron should be seasoned frequently, particularly

when your equipment is new. If rust occurs, clean with a heavy brush. Apply vegetable oil or shortening, and heat to season the grates. Note: certain grills have cast-iron grates coated with porcelain. The porcelain helps prevent rust and eliminates the need for seasoning.

Porcelain Wire Grates. There are special brushes on the market, such as Char-Broil's Brush Hawg, that can clean porcelain grates without scratching. After you finish cooking, turn heat to high for approximately 5 minutes; then use the brush to clean the grates after the grill has cooled.

Exterior Surfaces

For painted surfaces, warm soap and water work best. Some manufacturers offer an assortment of products for cleaning stainless-steel grills, from daily maintenance sprays and wipes to solutions that completely restore your grill's finish. Stainless-steel grills will develop rust if they are not protected from the outdoors. Check your owner's manual for detailed cleaning instructions.

Char-Broil Brush Hawg

GRILLING & BBQ ESSENTIALS

CB's Must-Have Pantry

■ **Pure Vegetable Oil/Cooking Oil Spray.** This is an essential tool for lubricating meat and grill grates.

■ **Kosher or Sea Salt.** The larger crystals of kosher or sea salt are wonderful because you can actually see where you have salted.

■ **Garlic (granulated and fresh).** This is a basic flavor for most grilling sauces and rubs.

■ **Cumin.** This spice is the secret of all great barbecue cooks.

■ **Onions (powdered, granulated, or fresh).** You'll find that onions enhance most every barbecue recipe.

■ **Apple Cider Vinegar.** This provides the flavor of apple cider without the sugar and is the choice of most master grillers. Use by itself as a spray or as a liquid component of wet rubs, mops, and sauces.

■ **Ketchup.** This versatile ingredient can be combined with many others to form a quick sauce.

■ **Brown Sugar.** I use it for dry rubs. When combined with ketchup, it creates a sweet glaze for pork or chicken. I even sprinkle a touch on steaks.

Char-Broil Spice Stick

CB's Essential Grilling Tools

■ **Knives.** A good knife is essential to prepping and carving meat. I recommend you choose knives that feel good in your hand, work for different tasks, can be used outdoors, don't cost a fortune, and are easy to clean and sharpen.

■ **Spatula.** I've tried all styles and price points, and my favorite has a wooden handle, a sturdy blade that supports a good-sized steak, and easily slides between the grate and the food. I use two spatulas to remove the skin from a side of salmon during grilling.

■ **Tongs.** I buy tongs in a variety of colors to indicate their purpose. I use red ones for raw meat and black ones for meat that's cooked.

■ **Fork.** I primarily use the fork with the tongs and spatula when I need a little extra help. I almost never use it to poke or turn meat.

■ **Basting Brush.** I am so grateful to the person who invented silicone cooking utensils. This type of brush is my mainstay. The angle is great for getting to places without twisting my wrist, and the brush holds sauce and clarified butter quite well.

■ **Thermometers.** The most important thermometer I own is a pocket instant-read thermometer. They are very useful for quickly testing meat in various areas to see if it's cooking evenly.

Char-Broil offers a remote digital thermometer that has both a food probe and a dangling device that reads the temperature right near the grates. It alerts me if the temperature inside the smoker starts to drop, and it keeps me informed of the internal temperature of the meat.

■ **Heat-Resistant Leather Gloves.** These bad boys are intended for heavy industrial use and can take sparks, heat, and hot metal. They aren't intended for playing in the fire but are very useful when you need to move hot grates and cast-iron pans, and when working around your grill, smoker, or barbecue.

CB'S FAVORITE BACKYARD COOKING TIPS

Great Burgers

The criteria for acclaiming a burger as "great" is regional in both flavor and style. However, the best burger in the world is the one I enjoy making and eating with my son on any given weekend. We use coarse-ground chuck—coarse because it holds together better, and chuck because it has great flavor.

A good fat-to-meat ratio is no more than 15 percent fat. More than that and your burger will drip fat, shrink, and cause flare-ups—unless, of course, you are using one of the new infrared gas grills, where you will notice fewer flare-ups and less meat shrinkage. Note: you can always buy a leaner ground beef and add a bit of olive oil.

Prepping the Patty. Using a wine bottle, gently press the ground chuck to about ¼ inch thick. Seasoning is a twist or two of freshly ground black pepper, a couple of pinches of sea or kosher salt, and our "secret" ingredients: ground cumin and finely minced fresh garlic. *Yeah baby—now yer talkin!*

After seasoning, fold the meat over, and gently press it down so it's about ½ inch thick. The seasoning is now in the middle of the patty, which evenly distributes the flavors. Use a pizza cutter to form patties out of the seasoned ground meat, making them just a bit larger than the size of the buns you plan to use. Store the patties in the refrigerator, chilling them to about 45°F until the grill is ready.

Grilling Rule #1—Make it HOT. Spritz the patties with a little canola oil as you take them out of the refrigerator, and put them directly on the grill to sear. I recommend a searing temperature of approximately 450°F. My infrared grill can deliver the heat to create great, restaurant-quality sear marks.

After the patties sear and are no longer sticking to the grates, use a metal spatula to turn and place them on a fresh part of the grill. After grill marks are established on both sides, remove patties to an aluminum pan or tray, cover with foil, and allow them to finish cooking from their residual heat. I like the meat seared on the outside and pink on the inside. (The USDA recommends an internal temperature of 160°F for ground beef, pork, lamb, and veal.) When using a conventional gas grill, brush patties with melted butter instead of canola oil before placing them on the grill.

Cheese Please! While the patties are finishing, I like to add thin slices of cheese or brush with BBQ sauce.

Cajun Burger, page 62

Succulent Steaks

Beef cuts with marbled fat throughout the meat will cook better over direct high heat. If you prefer to grill without removing the external fat, and your steak is less than 1 inch thick, cut or notch the fat about every 3 inches to help prevent the meat from curling. If you can afford them, prime and choice grades will give you a better value for flavor and quality. (Refer to the "Guide to Basic Beef Cuts" on page 297 for an overview of the best grill cuts.)

Marinades and Rubs. If I pay for a good cut of beef, I want to taste the meat, not the marinade or rub. However, some grill recipes call for seasoned or well-marinated beef. If you must marinate, remember that the acids in citrus fruit and vinegars will break down and tenderize the meat. Marinades containing sugar will quickly burn when exposed to high temperatures. The same holds true for rubs containing sugar.

Seasoning. I recommend a light sprinkle of freshly ground black pepper and kosher or sea salt. Some folks insist that salting a steak prior to cooking will dry it out. This is only partially true. Salt draws moisture from the steak, but that moisture is composed of naturally-occurring sugars and proteins. When these are exposed to searing temperatures, they brown and form the crust so many of us enjoy at a fine restaurant.

Searing. Searing the outside of a steak at a temperature in the range of 450°F to 550°F is the way professionals do it. Make sure you don't cook the steak at this temperature for the entire time, unless you enjoy meat that is crispy on the outside and raw on the inside. (See the cooking chart on page 297 to get a sense of correct time and temperatures.)

Steak on a Standard Gas Grill. Most folks cook their steaks at approximately 375°F to 400°F using a traditional convection gas grill. Charcoal grills can achieve temperatures of 400°F to 450°F. It requires temperatures of at least 450°F or more—similar to the heat used in a professional restaurant kitchen—to see grill

marks form on a rare steak. If your grill doesn't get quite this hot, lightly coat the outside of a seasoned steak with clarified butter or a touch of brown sugar.

Always turn steak with tongs or a spatula, not a fork. Check for doneness using an instant-read thermometer inserted in the side of the steak, preferably through any fat on the edge. (The USDA recommends 145°F for rare; 160°F for medium; and 170°F for well.)

Steak on an Infrared Gas Grill. Set the temperature on your infrared grill to high, and place the steaks on the grill, lined up in the same direction. Cook steaks on each side for 1 to 3 minutes to sear. Remove steaks; place them in an aluminum pan or tray; cover with foil or top with another pan; and place on a cooler section of the grill to finish cooking. Check for desired doneness with an instant-read thermometer.

Roasting. Another trick you'll see in a restaurant kitchen is to pull a steak from the grill, and place it in a pan in a 400°F oven. If you try this at home, watch the internal temperature of the steak to avoid overcooking.

Resting. After cooking, it's important to allow a steak to rest for about 10 minutes before slicing into it. This holding period keeps every bite juicy.

Char-Broil RED cooks with 100 percent infrared heat across the entire cooking surface.

Juicy Chicken

I may not be the world's authority on grilling chicken, but I do enjoy preparing and eating it. And over the years, I've acquired a few tricks that help ensure the most lip-smacking results.

Buy Fresh Chicken. Buy the best quality you can afford, and fresh is best. I've also taken to using organic chickens because I think they taste more like the chickens I remember eating as a kid.

To Brine or Not to Brine. My mom liked to tenderize chicken by soaking it overnight in buttermilk. Brine will produce the same results, and help retain juiciness. (See "CB's Basic Brine Recipe" on page 279.)

Seasoning. Apply sauces and glazes during the final minutes of cooking. If you like the taste of a dry rub, check the ingredient list before using. Many spices will burn when exposed to high temperatures, which can ruin the flavor. I recommend only a light seasoning of ground pepper, as well as kosher salt if the chicken hasn't been brined. You can also lightly spray chicken with canola oil to prevent sticking.

Temperature and Time. First, make sure to remove your chicken from the refrigerator and let it warm up for just a few minutes before cooking. Be careful never to let raw poultry reach room temperature, but try to avoid putting ice-cold chicken on the grill because that interferes with proper cooking.

The second most important rule for grilling chicken is to cook it from the inside out. The USDA recommends an internal temperature of 165°F for both chicken parts and whole chickens. Use an instant-read thermometer to gauge the internal temperature of the meat, making sure to keep the probe away from bones. If you cook chicken using the four-stage method suggested here, you can test the temperature at each stage.

Some things to remember: dark meat takes longer to cook than white meat; and larger pieces take longer to cook than smaller ones. The legs and thighs are dark meat. The wings, drumettes, and breast are white meat. Start cooking dark-meat chicken parts first. If you are cooking chicken halves, start them bone side down to speed up cooking.

Stage 1: Searing (450°F–550°F). This temperature range is perfect for searing steaks, and it's also a great place to start grilling chicken. A quick sear on both sides will help to lock in natural juices and flavor.

Stage 2: Grilling (350°F–450°F). On one-half of the grill, set the heat to medium-high (about 500°F). Set the heat to medium-low (about 375°F) on the other half. Start by placing fresh pieces of chicken on the hotter side. After searing for just a short time (2 to 3 minutes on an infrared grill, longer on a standard grill) the chicken will begin to get grill marks.

Although flare-ups on Char-Broil's infrared gas grills are rare, you may need to watch for them on other grills. Using your instant-read thermometer, check the chicken's internal temperature. Look for a temperature of approximately 145°F to 155°F to move from grilling to glazing.

Stage 3: Glazing (200°F). During the final ten minutes of cooking, reduce the heat under the chicken to low, and glaze the chicken with sauce. I like to use apricot or peach marmalade depending upon what else is on the menu. Whatever your taste dictates, the chicken should be almost fully cooked and removed from any direct heat before glazing. For perfect glazing, simmer the sauce before brushing it on the meat.

Stage 4: Rest, Rest, Rest. When you're finished grilling, place all of the chicken in trays or foil pans, cover, and let it rest for at least 10 minutes. This will help redistribute the juices inside each piece and allow the internal temperature to rise an additional 5 to 10 degrees. If you like, you may also add more sauce.

Tender, Moist Pork

Depending on the thickness, cut, and amount of fat, muscle, and bone, the cooking times for pork can vary considerably. Generally, 160˚F is considered a safe internal temperature for pork and yields a much juicier piece of meat.

Brining. Brining is similar to marinating because both methods involve soaking meat in a solution for several hours or overnight prior to cooking. Brining makes cooked meat more moist by hydrating the cells of the muscle tissue before cooking. You can brine pork shoulders, racks, roasts, and even chops. (You can find "CB's Basic Brine Recipe" on page 279.)

Injecting Flavors. Flavors and moisture can be added by injecting meat with marinade solutions before cooking. Needle injectors incorporate marinades directly into the thicker muscle of the meat. Here are additional tips to help you prepare pork.

■ Use an instant-read thermometer to check the internal temperature of the meat away from the bone and nearest to thickest part.

■ As you reach the end of the estimated cooking time, cut into the meat near the bone to determine doneness before pulling the meat off the grill. A pork chop is cooked when the meat is no longer pink near the bone.

■ Brush on glazes or sauces that contain sugar or honey during the last few minutes of grilling.

Smoked Pork Chops with Polenta and Cranberry Chutney, page 102

Lip-Smacking Pork Ribs

There are several varieties of ribs, and each requires a slightly different technique to bring out its best flavor and texture. Here are some general rules for ribs.

■ Apply a dry rub of herbs and spices before cooking.

■ Cook ribs for ½ to 1 hour depending on the amount of meat, bone, and fat they contain.

Q: "HOW LONG DO I COOK IT?" A: "UNTIL IT'S DONE."

This is the most common question I get from "Sizzle on the Grill" readers. The only honest answer I can give is that you need to learn from experience. Outdoor temperature, humidity, wind conditions, the thickness and type of meat, and the equipment you're using all factor into the finished product. Use the cooking times given in this book as a guide, and apply the USDA guidelines for safe internal food temperatures. (See chart on page 297.) Remember, however, that most cuts of meat will continue to cook after they are removed from the heat, rising an additional 5 to 10°F.

■ Baste the ribs with a light coating of apple cider vinegar during the last 10 minutes of cooking, or replace the vinegar with a glaze of marmalade or barbecue sauce.

■ On Char-Broil's infrared gas grills, you may drop wood chunks directly between the cooking grates. They will flavor the ribs but not actually smoke them.

■ Color is not necessarily an indication of when the rib is done. Smoke from burning wood chunks can turn the interior of the meat pink. Ribs are done when you can easily move the bones back and forth. To be certain, insert an instant-read thermometer into the thickest part of the meat away from the bone, measuring for an internal temperature of 160°F.

Delicious Vegetables

Grilling vegetables requires little preparation and imparts a delicious, lightly smoked flavor.

■ Set a standard gas grill to high; an infrared grill to medium-high.

■ Lightly brush or spray vegetables with olive oil before grilling to add flavor, promote sear marks, and keep them from sticking to the grill.

■ Some vegetables, such as corn on the cob, mushrooms, and baby eggplants, can be grilled whole. Others, such as zucchini, bell peppers,

and onions, should be sliced or cut into wedges.

■ Start vegetables over medium-high heat to sear their skins, turning every 1 to 2 minutes. Then move to low heat to finish cooking, turning occasionally.

■ The easiest way to tell if vegetables are cooked is to pierce them with a fork or skewer. If it goes in easily, the vegetables are done.

Savory Seafood

Grilling adds a smoky flavor to seafood and also gives it a crisp, savory crust. Whole fish, firm-flesh fish steaks and fillets, shrimp, and scallops are great on the grill. Hard-shelled mollusks, such as oysters, clams, and mussels, are often grilled in the shell, which causes the shell to open but does little to enhance the flavor.

■ Set a standard gas grill to high; an infrared grill to medium.

■ Before you begin, make sure the grill surface is clean and very hot before you begin to prevent sticking. Rub the grill quickly with a paper towel dipped in some oil before you add the seafood. (You can also use a grill basket or topper to grill seafood above the grill surface.)

■ Whole fish, such as snapper, pompano, and sea bass must be handled carefully to avoid sticking and

falling apart. Firm fish steaks, such as tuna, swordfish, and shark, are particularly good on the grill because they hold together well and don't stick.

■ Grilled shrimp are tastiest when the shell is left on. Lightly sprinkle the shrimp with salt, and grill for about 5 minutes until the shells turn pink.

Grilled Fruit for Dessert

Lightly grilling fruit—especially stone fruits, such as peaches, nectarines, apricots, and plums—caramelizes their natural sugars, enhances their flavor, and provides appetizing grill marks.

■ Set a standard gas grill to high; an infrared grill to medium.

■ Generously oil grill grate to avoid sticking.

■ Slice fruit in half and remove pits. Grill with pulp side down, turning once, until tender, about 3 to 5 minutes.

■ Fruit is done when it is lightly browned and tender but not mushy.

■ Fruit can burn easily because of its sugar content, so watch it closely.

■ Cut fruit, such as apples, pears, mangoes, pineapples, and peaches, into chunks and brush lightly with canola oil before grilling. Put pineapple or bananas sliced lengthwise directly on the grill.

2 Appetizers & Snacks

(Left) South-of-the-Border Pizza, page 52

AEGEAN GRILLED BRUSCHETTA

1 loaf French or Italian bread

2 tablespoons olive oil

3 ounces feta cheese, crumbled

2 ounces light cream cheese

2 teaspoons lemon juice

1 teaspoon fresh sage or oregano,
  finely chopped

1 7-ounce jar roasted red peppers,
  drained

1 cup pitted Italian or ripe olives,
  coarsely chopped

1 teaspoon olive oil

Small fresh sage or oregano
  leaves (optional)

Cut bread into 1-inch-thick slices. Lightly brush both sides of each slice with 2 tablespoons of olive oil.

Preheat grill to medium-high. Mix together feta cheese, cream cheese, lemon juice, and herbs. Cut red pepper into strips. Toss olives in remaining oil.

Place bread slices on grill; remove when bottom halves have toasted, approximately 2 to 3 minutes.

To assemble, spread toasted side of each piece of bread with cheese mixture. Top with red pepper strips, olives, and sage leaves. Arrange bread slices on lightly-oiled warming rack. Grill until other side of bread is slightly crisp and cheese on top has melted. ✤

SMOKED PECANS & GOUDA

1 pound pecan halves, walnuts, or almonds
⅓ cup butter, melted
Seasoned salt to taste
1½ pounds Gouda, shredded

With a small wooden skewer, punch several small holes in the bottom of a foil pan. Add pecans to melted butter and spread in an even layer in the pan. Sprinkle with seasoned salt. Add cheese to a second pan. Place both pans on the top rack of smoker. Smoke for 35 to 60 minutes. About halfway through cooking time, stir nuts and sprinkle with additional seasoned salt. Serve warm nuts and cheese with fruits and crackers. ✣

GRILLED SWEET-POTATO CHIPS

2 medium sweet potatoes,
    preferably red-skinned
Olive oil
Kosher salt

Peel sweet potatoes, and slice into ¼- to ½-inch-thick slices. Brush or spray lightly with olive oil. (For large quantities, place in a plastic zip-top bag; add the oil; and massage to coat all surfaces.) Season liberally with salt just before grilling.

Place potatoes directly on cooking grate over direct heat, and grill 3 minutes on each side or until seared. Move to indirect heat for about 20 minutes until tender; turn halfway through cooking time. When soft and tender, remove from grill; sprinkle with salt to taste, and serve immediately. ✤

GRILLED NACHOS

1 bag corn tortilla chips
1 small can sliced green chili peppers
4 ounces Monterey Jack cheese
4 ounces extra-sharp cheddar cheese
Sour cream
Salsa

Preheat grill to medium. Place tortilla chips in foil pan. Sprinkle chili peppers and cheeses on top.

Grill chips over medium heat with lid closed until melted, 10 to 12 minutes. Serve with sour cream and salsa. ✤

FRIED PICKLES

[*These delicious snacks, great with ice-cold beer,*
hail from the southern United States.]

Oil for frying

1 cup flour

1 cup yellow cornmeal

2 tablespoons favorite
   barbecue rub

¼ cup prepared yellow mustard

2 tablespoons beer

15–20 dill pickle slices

Heat oil in deep fryer to 350°F. In wide, flat pan, combine flour and cornmeal. Season mixture with barbecue rub. In a small bowl, mix mustard and beer. Dip pickle slices in mustard mixture; then in flour/cornmeal mix. Using tongs, carefully slip individual pickle slices into hot oil. Deep-fry until batter is browned. Pickles will float to top of hot oil when done. Remove from oil with tongs, and drain pickles on paper towels on a shallow plate. Serve hot. ♣

GEORGIA "CAVIAR"

2 cans whole-kernel corn, drained

1 can finely-diced tomatoes, drained

2 cans black-eyed peas, drained and rinsed

1 10-ounce bottle Italian dressing

2 cans diced tomatoes with green chilis

1 large red onion, finely diced

1 each red, green, and yellow bell pepper, finely diced

2 teaspoons salt

3 tablespoons cilantro, finely chopped

Tabasco to taste

Combine all ingredients; let set a minimum of 4 hours. (Overnight refrigeration is best.) Serve with your favorite dipping chips. Leftovers will keep for at least one week in refrigerator. ♣

GRILLED SPUDS WITH DIPPING SAUCE

4 large potatoes, peels on
Chives, minced
Bacon, cooked and crumbled

DIPPING SAUCE
¾ cup olive oil
3 tablespoons fresh lemon juice
1 large garlic clove, minced
1 tablespoon Parmesan, grated
1 teaspoon Worcestershire sauce
2 tablespoons chives, minced
Salt and freshly ground pepper

[*The dipping sauce is also great on salads.*]

Preheat oven to 400°F. Wash potatoes; rub with oil; then prick with fork. Bake 1 hour directly on oven rack, and remove from oven when tender. Cut potatoes in half lengthwise, and let cool. Scoop out center, leaving shell about ¼ inch thick. Reserve pulp for another use.

Preheat grill to medium. Whisk together dipping sauce ingredients in a small bowl. Brush potato skins lightly with dipping sauce, and grill for 3 to 4½ minutes per side, until crispy. Arrange skins on platter, and sprinkle with chives and bacon. Serve warm with dipping sauce. ✤

STUFFED MUSHROOMS ON THE GRILL

24 large mushrooms, cleaned
  and stems removed
2 tablespoons butter
2 teaspoons onion, minced

¾ cup sharp cheese, shredded
⅓ cup bacon bits
⅓ cup bread crumbs
2 tablespoons parsley, chopped
1 to 2 tablespoons sherry
  (optional)

Preheat grill to medium. Mix stuffing ingredients together; stuff mushroom with mixture.

Cut six squares of heavy-duty aluminum foil. Wrap four mushrooms in each square of foil; seal; and place on grill. Grill 12 to 15 minutes without turning packets. Serve while hot. ✦

2

APPETIZERS & SNACKS

TIM BARR'S NO-MAYO DEVILED EGGS WITH SMOKED APPLE AND CHIPOTLE

1 small apple

3 to 4 jalapeño peppers

1 dozen eggs, hardboiled, shells removed

¼ cup peppercorn ranch dressing

2 tablespoons Dijon mustard

2 tablespoons sour cream

1 tablespoon bread-and-butter pickle juice

In smoker or grill, smoke apple and jalapeños at 350°F for 5 to 10 minutes. (Don't let apple soften.) Finely chop apple and jalapeños, and set aside. Slice eggs in half; remove yolks; and place yolks in a small bowl. Add dressing, mustard, sour cream, and pickle juice, mixing well. Once mixture is creamy, add finely chopped apple and chipotles. Mix again until evenly incorporated. Pipe or spoon mixture into whites and serve. ♣

Charlotte, North Carolina, native Tim Barr has been stationed all over the world as a U.S. Coast Guard officer. He missed authentic barbecue so much that he began inventing his own recipes.

CB'S EASY SMOKY CHICKEN DRUMETTES PARTY PLATTER

20 chicken wing drumettes
2 tablespoons garlic powder
1 teaspoon ground ginger
1 teaspoon ground mustard
1 pinch ground cumin
Coarse salt & pepper to taste
¼ cup peanut or canola oil
¼ cup white wine
¼ cup favorite BBQ sauce for dipping

Rinse and pat dry chicken drumettes, and place them in a large mixing bowl. Add the next five ingredients, and mix thoroughly. Drizzle oil onto drumettes, and mix until chicken is lightly coated with oil and spices.

Preheat grill to high. Place small packet of moist wood chips on grill; when they begin to smoke, reduce heat to medium.

Grill chicken approximately 8 to 10 minutes, turning to prevent burning. Keep lid closed between turns to ensure that the smoke permeates the meat. After drumettes have browned sufficiently, remove them from grill, and place them in the center of a large sheet of aluminum foil. Fold foil around the drumettes, leaving a small opening. Pour wine into opening, and loosely seal foil. Place foil packet with drumettes back onto grill until wine begins to steam. Remove drumettes, and garnish with lettuce, celery, or parsley. Serve with your favorite BBQ sauce. ✤

MEN IN APRONS'
SPICY MAPLE GRILLED WINGS

1 package (18–24) chicken wings
½ teaspoon each of salt, pepper, and paprika
¼ cup pure maple syrup
3 tablespoons brown sugar
1 tablespoon butter
3 tablespoons Thai chili sauce

Mix together salt, pepper, and paprika; then season wings. Preheat one side of grill to medium, the other side to low. In small saucepan, add syrup, sugar, butter, and chili sauce. Bring to a simmer, whisking briskly. Remove from heat. Grill wings for 2 to 3 minutes per side over medium heat; then transfer them to low heat burner. Continue cooking over this burner, turning occasionally, for about 20 minutes or until skin is nicely browned and crisp. About 2 minutes before removing them from the grill, brush wings with maple glaze. Serve.✦

Adam Byrd is a self-taught grilling and cooking enthusiast from Round Rock, Texas. He publishes a popular online recipe site called "Men In Aprons" and regularly participates in new product testing for Char-Broil.

BACON-WRAPPED SCALLOPS

1 pound bacon slices, halved
¾ cup butter, melted
2 tablespoons lemon juice
1 teaspoon salt
⅛ teaspoon pepper
1½ pounds large scallops
Sesame seeds

Preheat grill to medium. Partially cook bacon. Combine butter, lemon juice, salt, and pepper. Add scallops, and toss until well coated. Wrap each scallop in one slice of bacon (two smaller scallops may be wrapped in one bacon slice); secure with toothpick. Coat each with sesame seeds. Place scallops in oiled grill basket or on skewers, and grill over medium fire, turning once, for about 10 minutes or until bacon is crisp. ♣

BACON-WRAPPED BARBECUED SHRIMP

1 pound large, giant, or jumbo
   shrimp, shelled and deveined

1 slice of bacon per shrimp, partially
   cooked, cut in half

1 each red and yellow bell pepper,
   seeded, cleaned, and cut in 1-inch
   chunks

1 small olive per shrimp

1 cup of your favorite barbecue sauce

Grilling basket, or 8 bamboo skewers,
   soaked for 2 hours

Fresh lime juice

Place an olive in center of each shrimp, and wrap a piece of bacon around each shrimp. Place one or two pieces of pepper on each skewer, followed by one bacon-wrapped shrimp. Coat with barbecue sauce, and place over direct heat for 3 minutes. If using larger shrimp, you may need to cook an additional 2 to 3 minutes until shrimp turns opaque. Drizzle with lime juice. Serve. ✤

CB'S EASY GRILLED "TAPAS" SANDWICHES

1 loaf crusty country-style bread

4 tablespoons butter, melted

Assorted vegetables (such as eggplant, zucchini, onions, peppers, and lettuce)

Sliced cheeses

Thinly-sliced cold cuts

Preheat grill to high. Cut bread into medium-thick slices. Cut vegetables into thin slices, making sure slices are large enough not to fall through the grill grates. Slice cheeses and meats into appropriate size for bread.

Brush vegetables with olive oil; grill about 3 minutes per side, and remove. Cover and keep warm.

Place bread slices on grill and lightly brown one side; then turn and brush browned side with butter. Brown other side. Remove bread, and cover to keep warm.

Cover grill with aluminum foil. Turn heat to medium. After foil is warm, place meat slices directly on sheet to warm. Remove and keep warm. Add cheese slices to toasted bread. Place on sheet; then close lid for 2 to 3 minutes. This will warm bread and slightly melt cheese.

Open grill and layer bread with warmed meat and grilled vegetables. Serve on warmed plates with condiments. ✤

2

APPETIZERS & SNACKS

CB'S EZ GRILLED ASPARAGUS SOUP

2–3 garlic cloves, unpeeled

Olive oil

2–4 pounds asparagus, washed and trimmed of tough ends

1 large yellow or sweet onion, chopped

Freshly ground pepper and kosher salt

Chicken stock or vegetable broth (1 cup per serving)

1–2 tablespoons of flour or cornstarch

1 tablespoons unsalted butter

¼ cup light cream or whole milk

[*Instead of cooking asparagus and onions in a stockpot, I prefer to grill them. The charring adds a wonderfully smoky taste.* —CB]

Preheat grill to medium high. Oil unpeeled garlic cloves; wrap in aluminum foil; and place on heating rack of grill for about 30 minutes. When garlic is soft, remove from heat. Peel; then mash garlic in a small bowl, and set aside.

Lightly coat asparagus and onions with oil and season with pepper and salt. Place on grill. Using long tongs, turn vegetables often to create grill marks, but be careful not to burn them. Remove when done.

In blender, puree grilled asparagus and onions, gradually adding ½ cup of chicken stock to help liquefy. Place puree into a large stockpot, and simmer for about 25 minutes, adding more stock if necessary. Stir in flour, butter, cream, and roasted garlic. Simmer for about an hour to allow flavors to meld. If desired, strain soup through a sieve for a smoother texture. Ladle into individual bowls or cups. Garnish with grilled asparagus tips. ✦

GRILLED COUNTRY CORN BREAD

1 cup all-purpose flour

1 cup yellow or white
  cornmeal

1 teaspoon sugar

2 teaspoons baking
  powder

1 teaspoon sea salt

1 large egg

1 cup milk

⅛ cup olive oil, melted
  butter, or bacon drippings

1 heaping cup
  canned creamed corn

6 pieces of bacon, cooked
  crisp and cut into pieces
  (optional)

2 tablespoons butter

Mix the flour and cornmeal. Add the sugar, baking powder, and salt. Using a wire whisk, mix until well combined, and set aside. In a separate bowl, mix the egg, milk, and oil. Add the wet ingredients to the dry ingredients, and mix until just combined. Add the creamed corn and the bacon, if using; mix until just combined. Do not over mix. Set aside.

Preheat grill to high. Place a 10-inch cast-iron skillet on the center of the cooking grate. When skillet is hot, add 2 table-spoons of butter. Once butter melts, pour the batter directly into the skillet. Cover grill, and cook over indirect high heat—about 450°F—for 35 to 40 minutes or until a toothpick comes out clean when placed in the center. Cut and serve corn bread right from the pan while still warm. ✦

CHEESY GRILLED CHICKEN QUESADILLAS

1 3-ounce package cream cheese, softened

1 cup Monterey Jack cheese, shredded

⅓ cup feta cheese, crumbled

½ teaspoon dried oregano

4 large flour tortillas

1 large grilled chicken breast, chopped

⅓ cup pitted ripe olives, chopped

2 tablespoons pimento, diced

2 tablespoons green onion, thinly sliced

For filling, stir together cream cheese, Monterey Jack, feta, and oregano. Spread ¼ of the filling onto half of each tortilla. Top with chicken, olives, pimento, and green onion. Fold plain side over; press gently to seal edges. Preheat grill to high; then reduce to medium. Place tortillas on grill, flipping once. When cheese has melted (about 5 to 8 minutes), remove and cut into three wedges. Serve immediately. ☘

SPICY GRILLED VEGETABLE QUESADILLAS

1 each red, yellow, and green bell pepper, seeded and halved

1 red onion, cut into ½-inch slices

¾ cup olive oil

¾ cup fresh cilantro, chopped

2 tablespoons fresh lemon juice

Salt and black pepper

¾ cup Colby or Monterey Jack cheese, shredded

¾ cup sharp cheddar cheese, shredded

1 tablespoon cayenne pepper

1 tablespoon oregano

1 tablespoon garlic powder

8 flour tortillas (8- to 10-inch)

Preheat grill to medium. Brush pepper halves and onions with olive oil; grill over medium heat until tender. Cool; then coarsely chop. In bowl, combine chopped pepper and onions, cilantro, lemon juice, and salt and pepper to taste. Combine cheeses, cayenne pepper, oregano, and garlic powder. Brush tortillas with olive oil. Place four tortillas on grill surface over low heat. Spread pepper/onion mixture to cover tortilla; then sprinkle liberally with cheese mixture. When bottom of tortilla is brown, place another tortilla over top of each. With wide spatula, carefully turn quesadilla, and continue to grill until golden brown. Slice into wedges, and serve with tomato salsa. ✤

GRILLED CHILI-CHEESE BREAD

1 loaf French bread

½ cup mayonnaise

2 cups cheddar or Monterey Jack cheese, shredded

1 teaspoon chili powder

¼ cup green chilies, chopped

½ teaspoon ground cumin

Preheat grill to medium low. Slice bread diagonally, but don't cut through bottom. Combine mayonnaise, cheese, chili powder, chilies, and cumin in a bowl. Spread mixture over cut surfaces of bread. Wrap in foil. Grill over medium-low heat (350°F) for 15 to 20 minutes, turning occasionally until heated through. ✤

CRAN-GERINE UPSIDE-DOWN BISCUITS

¼ **cup butter, melted**

1 **16-ounce can whole berry cranberry sauce**

2 **teaspoons tangerine or orange zest, grated**

¼ **cup chopped pecans**

1 **teaspoon ground cinnamon**

1 **10-count can refrigerated biscuits**

Preheat oven to 400°F. Combine butter, cranberry sauce, tangerine zest, pecans, and cinnamon in a medium bowl. Divide mixture between 10 greased muffin tins; top with biscuits. Bake for 12 to 15 minutes. Cool 5 minutes; run knife around edges; and invert pan onto platter. ✤

Bev Jones of Brunswick, Missouri, won first prize in the 2007 Char-Broil Thanksgiving Recipe Contest for this holiday breakfast treat.—CB

WILD MUSHROOM PITA PIZZA

5 button mushrooms, sliced

2 shiitake mushrooms, sliced

2 oyster mushrooms, sliced

1 large portabella mushroom, sliced

2 tablespoons red onion, diced

½ each red and green bell pepper,
   julienned

2 cloves garlic, crushed

¼ cup white wine

¼ cup chicken broth

2 pocketless pita breads

1 cup tomato sauce

1 cup mixed cheese, shredded

Preheat grill to medium-low. Place one or two sheets of aluminum foil over grill grates. Add mushrooms, onion, and peppers to medium saucepan with garlic, wine, and chicken stock; sauté for 5 to 7 minutes. Drain liquid. Cover pita with tomato sauce. Add mushroom mixture; then sprinkle with cheese. Place on tin foil over medium-low grill until cheese melts. ✤

BASIC PIZZA DOUGH

½ cup cold milk

½ cup hot water

1 package active dry yeast

Pinch sugar

2¼ teaspoons kosher salt

1 tablespoon extra-virgin
   olive oil

¼ cup cornmeal

2¾ cups flour

Combine milk and water in a large bowl. Add yeast and sugar; set aside until yeast foams. Stir in salt, oil, and cornmeal. Gradually stir in flour until soft dough forms. Turn dough out onto floured surface; knead until smooth and shiny, about 10 minutes. Return dough to greased bowl; cover tightly with oiled plastic wrap; and let rise about 2 hours or until doubled in size.

Press dough down gently, and proceed with your favorite grilled pizza or grilled bread recipe. Yields two pizzas.

Tip: Be sure to work on a well-floured surface and to flour rolling pin to prevent dough from sticking. Shape pie as evenly and thinly as possible but not so thin that holes appear in dough. Some prefer crust that is less than ¼ inch thick; others prefer it thicker. When set on grill, dough firms up immediately and thickens slightly. Not all pies will conform to a perfectly round shape. Free-form shapes are completely acceptable when making homemade pizza. ✤

CB'S BEST GRILLED PIZZA

1 pizza dough recipe (see page 48), or
  premade dough
Cornmeal for dusting pan
¼ cup extra-virgin olive oil
4 cloves garlic, minced
¼ cup Parmesan cheese, freshly grated
1 cup mozzarella cheese, shredded
1 cup Italian-style tomato sauce
Fresh basil leaves cut into strips

VARIATIONS

- Sliced pepperoni and Canadian bacon
- Grilled portabella mushrooms and asparagus
- Sautéed peppers and onions
- Fresh or frozen spinach with ground sausage or prosciutto
- Crisp bacon or grilled ham cubes and artichoke hearts
- Goat cheese and sun-dried tomatoes or cherry tomatoes
- Smoked salmon, chives, and sour cream
- Grilled eggplant and goat cheese
- Cooked ground beef, shrimp, scallops, or clams, with chopped fresh tomatoes, garlic, and basil

Scatter handful of cornmeal over pizza pans. On a lightly floured surface, divide dough into two portions; form each into a smooth ball; then press each ball with hands to flatten. Gently stretch each round into a disk about ½ inch thick and 8 inches across. Using a flour-dusted rolling pin, roll out each disk to about ⅛ inch thick—dusting surface with additional flour if necessary—until dough measures 12 to 14 inches in diameter.

Place dough on pizza pans, and shake to cover bottoms with cornmeal. If dough sticks anywhere, lift edge gently and sprinkle more cornmeal underneath.

Preheat grill to medium. Slide first pan onto grill, and cook until lightly browned, about 4 minutes. Pop any bubbles with tongs. Remove pan from grill; flip dough over. Return to grill, and cook about 30 seconds more until just set. Remove from grill, and repeat steps with second pizza.

Brush both pizzas with olive oil; scatter on garlic; sprinkle on cheeses; dab on tomato sauce; and sprinkle on basil. Return to grill, and close lid. Cook about 4 minutes or until cheese is melted and bottom crust is browned. ✣

SOUTH-OF-THE-BORDER CHICKEN PIZZA

1 pizza dough recipe (See page 48.)
2 cloves garlic, minced
1 cup fresh cilantro, chopped
⅓ cup fresh Parmesan cheese, grated
6 tablespoons olive oil
Salt and freshly ground black pepper
1¼ cup Monterey Jack cheese, grated
1½ cup grilled chicken breast, shredded
2 ripe plum tomatoes, sliced or chopped
½ cup fresh green chilies, chopped
Crushed red pepper to taste

Prepare pizza dough recipe, adding one clove minced garlic. Preheat grill to high. In food processor, pulse together cilantro, one clove garlic, and Parmesan. Slowly pour in oil until combined and mixture resembles pesto. Add salt and pepper to taste. Reserve for pizza assembly.

When grill is hot, place first pizza crust directly onto oiled grill grates; cook 1 to 1½ minutes until crust becomes somewhat firm. Flip crust over onto baking sheet with cooked side up. Spread half of pesto mixture on top; then sprinkle with half of Monterey Jack cheese, chicken, tomatoes, green chilies, and crushed red pepper.

Slide pizza off baking sheet back onto grill; placing it so half is over high heat and other half is over medium to low heat. Cook pizza 3 to 4 minutes, rotating frequently to get uniformly brown, crisp crust. Slide pizza onto a serving board, and slice into wedges. Repeat process for second pizza. Yields two 10-inch pizzas. ✤

2

APPETIZERS & SNACKS

CAJUN-STYLE PIZZA

1 pizza dough recipe (See page 48.)

1 clove garlic, minced

1 pound Andouille sausage, grilled and chopped

2 cups mozzarella cheese, shredded

½ cup scallions, grilled and chopped

1 cup roasted peppers, chopped

½ teaspoon ground thyme

½ teaspoon ground coriander

½ teaspoon cumin

½ teaspoon paprika

1 tablespoon dried parsley

Freshly ground black pepper to taste

Tabasco sauce to taste

Prepare pizza dough with minced garlic added. Preheat grill to high. Transfer first pizza crust to grill. Grill uncovered over high heat for 1 to 1½ minutes. Flip crust onto baking sheet, cooked side up. Top with half of sausage, mozzarella, scallions, and roasted peppers. Mix next six dry ingredients together in a small container; shake well to blend. Sprinkle half of seasonings on top of first pizza. Top with a few drops of Tabasco sauce to taste. Transfer pizza back to grill, and cook for another 3 minutes or until cheese melts. Repeat process for second pizza. ♣

INDONESIAN HANGER STEAK SATÉ

20–30 short bamboo skewers

1 pound hanger steak cut into
   1-inch strips

2 teaspoon fresh ginger, grated

½ teaspoon turmeric

2 tablespoons tamari or
   soy sauce

2 teaspoons honey

1 teaspoon lime juice

½ ground black pepper

¼ teaspoon red pepper flakes

¼ teaspoon salt

2 tablespoons canola oil

[*This recipe is courtesy of Emmy Award-nominated chef, television host, restaurateur, and cookbook author Marvin Woods.*]

Soak skewers in cold water for approximately 1 hour before cooking. Preheat grill to high. Combine beef, ginger, turmeric, tamari, honey, lime juice, black pepper, red pepper, salt, and canola oil. Take a piece of hanger steak, and thread meat onto skewer, forming an "S" shape.

If concerned about sticking, spray oil directly onto grill or use a cloth and brush the grill with oil. Place skewers on grill, keeping meat over fire, taking care not to expose whole skewer to heat. Cook 3 to 5 minutes. Marinade adds enough flavor so you don't need sauce. ✤

2

APPETIZERS & SNACKS

KANSAS CITY WARM-YOU-UP CHILI

1 pound chopped beef
½ cup onion, chopped
1 16-ounce can red beans
1 16-ounce can refried beans
1 8-ounce can tomato sauce
1 cup water
3 tablespoons chili powder

1 tablespoon molasses
1 teaspoon red pepper
  flakes
½ teaspoon salt
½ teaspoon garlic salt
⅛ teaspoon pepper
⅛ teaspoon cayenne

This rib-sticking recipe is courtesy of the Kansas City Barbecue Society, which has 8,000 international members.

Brown chopped beef with onion in heavy sauce pan; drain. Add red beans, refried beans, tomato sauce, water, chili powder, molasses, red pepper, salt, garlic salt, pepper, and cayenne; mix well. Simmer covered for 3 to 4 hours or until desired consistency, stirring occasionally. ⚜

BILL'S STUFFED BELL PEPPERS IN THE BIG EASY

4–6 firm bell peppers, tops and seeds removed
1 pound favorite meatloaf recipe

Place unstuffed peppers cut-side up in a glass dish filled with about 1 inch of water. Cover with plastic wrap, and microwave on high for 2 minutes.

Stuff peppers with favorite meatloaf recipe. (The amount depends upon the size of each pepper.) Place stuffed peppers in the bottom of the wire cooking basket. Insert thermometer probe in one pepper, and turn on the burner. After about 10 to 15 minutes, put mesh lid on cooker to give tops of stuffing a little crispiness.

When thermometer shows 160°F (approximately 45 minutes), remove basket and set inside on counter. Let cooked peppers rest for about 5 to 7 minutes before serving. ♣

It's a cinch to cook these stuffed peppers in The Big Easy. The pepper skins roast to perfection, and the stuffing mixture cooks all the way through. Best of all, you don't need to use a drop of oil!—CB

2

APPETIZERS & SNACKS

3
Beef, Lamb & Veal

(Left) Cajun Burgers, page 62

⊕ **Quick Meal • 6 Servings • Prep: 20 min. • Grill: 10 min.**

HOLY GUACAMOLE BURGERS

2 to 3 heads of garlic, roasted (See page 289.)

Vegetable oil

2 cups mayonnaise

½ teaspoon lemon juice

2 pounds ground chuck

1 tablespoon Worcestershire sauce

1 teaspoon coarse salt

½ teaspoon freshly ground black pepper

2 tablespoons Tex-Mex Rub (See below.)

6 thick slices ripe tomato

6 lettuce leaves

6 large hamburger buns

Guacamole (see page 293), or pre-made

Salt and freshly ground pepper to taste

Mix all ingredients for the Tex-Mex Rub in a small bowl. Set aside.

For garlic mayonnaise, squeeze one bulb roasted garlic from its skin into a medium bowl. Using fork, mash garlic, pressing against side of bowl. Add mayonnaise and lemon juice, and mix well. Refrigerate mixture until ready to serve burgers.

Place second bulb of roasted garlic in a large bowl, and mash with fork against side of bowl. Add ground chuck, Worcestershire sauce, salt, and pepper, and mix with hands until just combined. Gently form six patties approximately ½ to ¾ inches thick. Coat patties with dry rub.

Preheat grill to high. Grill burgers for approximately 1 minute on each side. Reduce grill temperature to medium, and continue cooking burgers for 4 to 5 minutes more per side. Toast buns at edge of grill. Spread garlic mayonnaise on one half of each bun, and top with lettuce, burger, guacamole, and tomato slice. Sprinkle with salt and pepper. ⊛

TEX-MEX RUB

2 tablespoons chili powder	2 teaspoons ground cumin
4 teaspoons garlic salt	1½ teaspoons dried oregano
2½ teaspoons onion powder	¾ teaspoon cayenne pepper

BEER BURGERS SMASHED WITH FRESH GOAT CHEESE

1½ pounds ground beef

1 teaspoon salt

2 tablespoons onion, minced

6 slices goat cheese, chilled until firm

⅓ can beer

3 tablespoons steak sauce

⅓ cup ketchup

1 tablespoon prepared mustard

1 tablespoon sugar

6 hamburger or potato buns, buttered

Combine first three ingredients, and shape meat into half patties. Place slice of goat cheese on one half; then put another half patty on top to form whole burger.

Combine next five ingredients, and heat in a saucepan until mixture thickens. Keep warm.

Preheat grill to high. Place patties in an oiled grill basket; grill 4 to 6 minutes on each side. Toast hamburger buns on edge of grill, turning once, for approximately 2 minutes.

Place beef patties in buns, and top with warm sauce before serving. ✺

CAJUN BURGERS

2 pounds ground beef

1 cup seasoned breadcrumbs

2 tablespoons ground coriander

2 tablespoons Cajun spice

¼ teaspoon dried steak seasoning

¼ teaspoon dried oregano

1 teaspoon Worcestershire sauce

¼ teaspoon garlic powder

2 jalapeño peppers, seeded
   and diced

Combine all ingredients in a large mixing bowl with ground beef; form into patties (6–8 ounces each).

Cook on high heat until desired doneness, 6–8 minutes per side for medium. ✳

CB'S INSIDE-OUT & UPSIDE-DOWN BURGERS

1 pound lean ground beef

6 strips lean bacon, cooked but
not crisp, chopped

1 cup shredded cheese mix,
such as cheddar and jack
cheese

3 tablespoons olive oil

½ teaspoon Worcestershire sauce

1 clove garlic, minced

4 tablespoons unsalted butter

2 teaspoons sea salt or kosher salt

Freshly ground black pepper

In a large mixing bowl, gently fold together ground beef, bacon, cheese, olive oil, Worcestershire sauce, and garlic. Form mixture into three round balls. Gently press burger balls into 1- to 2-inch-thick patties. Chill for at least 30 minutes.

Preheat the grill to high. Melt butter in a small saucepan. Remove burgers from the refrigerator; season with salt and pepper to taste.

Lightly brush one side of each burger with melted butter; place, buttered-side down, on one side of grill; and reduce heat on that side to medium, leaving other side of grill on high. Cook for approximately 7 minutes with lid closed.

Open lid, and brush top of burgers with remaining butter. Using an oiled spatula, gently lift patties; place, buttered side down, on opposite side of grill over high heat. Reduce heat on that side to medium and close lid. Cook for 5 minutes. Let patties rest, covered with foil, for approximately 2 minutes. Place on buns, and serve. ✸

BBQ CHUCK STEAK

**1½ pounds beef chuck, cut into
   ¾- to 1-inch-thick slices**

MARINADE
**1 cup finely chopped onion
1 cup ketchup
⅓ cup packed brown sugar
⅓ cup red wine vinegar
1 tablespoon Worcestershire sauce
⅛ teaspoon crushed red pepper**

Combine marinade ingredients in a medium bowl. Place steak and 1 cup of marinade in food-safe plastic bag; turn to coat. Refrigerate remaining marinade.

Close bag securely. Marinate steak in refrigerator 6 hours or as long as overnight, turning occasionally. Remove steak; discard marinade. Place steak on the grill over medium heat. Grill, uncovered, 15 to 18 minutes for medium-rare to medium, turning occasionally.

Place refrigerated marinade in a small saucepan; bring to a boil. Reduce heat; simmer 10 to 15 minutes or until sauce thickens slightly, stirring occasionally.

Cut steak into serving-size pieces. Serve with sauce. ✹

4–6 Servings • Prep: 20 min. • Marinate: 6 hr.–overnight • Grill: 15 min.

65

CAESAR SKIRT STEAK WITH CHUNKY OLIVE TAPENADE

⅔ cup Kalamata and/or green pimento-stuffed olives, chopped

½ cup prepared non-creamy Caesar dressing, divided

2 teaspoons freshly grated lemon peel

1 teaspoon minced garlic

1 skirt or flank steak, (1½ to 2 pounds)

Combine olives, 1 tablespoon dressing, lemon peel, and garlic in small bowl; season with pepper. Cover and refrigerate until ready to use.

Place meat and remaining dressing in a food-safe plastic bag; turn steak to coat. Close bag securely, and let marinate in refrigerator 6 hours or as long as overnight, turning occasionally.

Remove steak; discard marinade. Place steak on grill over medium heat. Grill, uncovered, 10 to 13 minutes, (17 to 21 minutes if using flank steak) for medium-rare to medium, turning occasionally.

Carve steak across the grain into thin slices. Serve with olive mixture. ✹

STEAK & POTATO KABOBS

1 pound all-purpose potatoes

1 medium yellow or zucchini squash

1 pound boneless top sirloin steak, cut into 1-inch-thick cubes

SAUCE

¾ cup Heinz 57 Sauce

2 large cloves garlic, minced

Cut potatoes into 1½-inch pieces. Place in a microwave-safe dish; cover with vented plastic wrap. Microwave on high 6 to 8 minutes or until just tender, stirring once. Cool slightly.

Combine sauce ingredients in 1-cup glass measure. Microwave on high 1½ minutes, stirring once.

Cut steak and squash into 1¼-inch pieces. Combine beef, squash, potatoes, and ⅓-cup sauce in a large bowl; toss. Alternately thread beef and vegetables onto metal skewers.

Place kabobs on grill over medium heat. Grill, uncovered, approximately 10 to 12 minutes for medium-rare to medium, turning occasionally. Brush kabobs with remaining sauce during last 5 minutes. ✹

HAPPY "HOLLA" BRANDY PEPPER STEAK

1 2-pound sirloin steak, 1½ to 2
   inches thick

2 teaspoons coarsely ground pepper

½ cup beef bouillon

1½ teaspoons salt

½ cup Slivovitz (plum brandy)
   or regular brandy

1 teaspoon cornstarch

2 tablespoons water

8 ounces mushrooms, cleaned and
   sliced (optional)

[*Ed Roith, of the Happy "Holla" Bar-B-Q team of Shawnee, Kansas, created this steak recipe, which is cooked in a skillet on top of the grill.*]

Trim excess fat from steak and reserve. Render some of the fat in a large skillet that has been preheated on the grill over high heat.

Reduce heat to medium-high. Sprinkle both sides of steak with pepper, and add to skillet. Cook until browned on each side. Reduce heat, and cook for 8 to 10 minutes. Remove steak to warm platter.

Drain pan drippings, reserving 2 teaspoons. Combine reserved drippings, bouillon, salt, and brandy in skillet. Add mushrooms, and cook until reduced by one-quarter, stirring constantly. Stir in cornstarch mixed with water. Cook until thickened, continuing to stir.

Slice steak thinly across grain. Pour mixture over steak. ❄

3

BEEF, LAMB & VEAL

EASY MARINATED FLANK STEAK

Flank steak (1½ pounds)
½ cup any hickory-flavored
barbecue sauce
¼ cup red wine

Place steak in a large zip-top plastic bag. Combine barbecue sauce with red wine; pour mixture over steak. Seal bag, and turn several times to coat steak. Marinate 4 to 24 hours in refrigerator, turning several times.

Discard marinade. Grill steak over medium heat to desired doneness, turning and brushing with additional barbecue sauce. ❀

MONTREAL GRILLED T-BONE

½ cup beef stock

½ diced onion

½ teaspoon chili flakes

½ cup chicken broth

2 ounces bourbon

1 ounce port

4 14-ounce T-bone steaks

¼ teaspoon Cajun seasoning

Salt and pepper to taste

Combine first six ingredients in medium sauce pan. Bring to a boil. Simmer uncovered 4 minutes.

Sprinkle steaks with Cajun seasoning, salt, and pepper. Cook steaks on high heat until desired doneness. Place steaks on plate. Serve with sauce. ❁

PORTERHOUSE WITH SPICY PARMESAN BUTTER

1 Porterhouse steak (approximately 3 inches thick)

¼ cup olive oil

8 garlic cloves, minced

1 tablespoon fresh thyme, chopped

1 tablespoon salt

2 teaspoons ground black pepper

1½ teaspoons fresh rosemary, chopped

Spicy Parmesan Butter (See recipe.)

2 Servings • Prep: 30 min. • Marinate: 2 hr.–overnight • Grill: 40 min.

71

SPICY PARMESAN BUTTER

3 tablespoons butter, room temperature

2 teaspoons grated Parmesan cheese

1 anchovy fillet, drained and minced

1 teaspoon paprika

½ teaspoon Dijon mustard

½ teaspoon Worcestershire sauce

¼ teaspoon ground black pepper

¼ teaspoon Tabasco sauce

Prepare butter by mixing all ingredients in a small bowl until blended. (Can be made 2 days ahead.) Refrigerate. When ready to use, remove from refrigerator and warm to room temperature.

Place steak in a glass dish. Whisk oil and next 5 ingredients in a small bowl to blend. Pour half of marinade over steak. Turn steak over, and coat with remaining marinade. Cover and refrigerate at least 2 hours and up to 24 hours, turning steak occasionally.

Preheat grill to medium. Remove meat from marinade, and grill to desired doneness or until internal temperature reaches 115°F to 130°F for medium-rare, approximately 18 minutes per side. Transfer steak to a platter; cover; and let rest for 5 minutes.

Cutting away from bone, slice each meat section into ⅓-inch slices. Spread Spicy Parmesan Butter over each portion, and serve. ✽

CB'S GRILLED NY STRIP STEAK

2 8-ounce New York strip steaks, approximately 1 inch thick

2 teaspoons kosher salt or sea salt

1 teaspoon freshly ground black pepper

2 tablespoons butter or oil

Trim steaks of any excess fat and allow to rest, covered loosely with wax paper, for 15 minutes at room temperature.

Preheat a gas grill to high or until coals are white hot on a charcoal grill. Season steaks with salt and pepper; then brush steaks lightly on both sides with melted butter or oil.

Grill steaks for approximately 5 minutes. Turn once using a spatula, and cook for an additional 2 to 5 minutes, depending upon thickness.

Check for doneness using an instant-read thermometer (145°F for medium rare). Remove steaks to a warm platter, and allow to rest for at least 2 minutes before serving. ✽

🕐 Quick Meal • 2 Servings • Prep: 10–20 min. • Grill: 15 min.

73

GRILLED TENDERLOINS WITH BLUE CHEESE TOPPING

2 tenderloin steaks, approximately ½ pound each
1 large clove garlic, halved
½ teaspoon salt
½ teaspoon fresh parsley, chopped

TOPPING

2 tablespoons cream cheese
4 teaspoons crumbled blue cheese
4 teaspoons plain yogurt
2 teaspoons minced onion
Dash ground white pepper

Combine topping ingredients in a small bowl. Rub steaks with garlic halves.

Place steaks on hot grill, and cook 8 to 11 minutes, turning occasionally. One to two minutes before steaks are done, season with salt; then top evenly with cheese mixture. Remove from grill; sprinkle with parsley; and serve. ✺

BLOODY MARY LONDON BROIL

2 cups tomato juice

¼ cup Worcestershire sauce

3 tablespoons prepared horseradish

3 tablespoons dry sherry

2 teaspoons dried marjoram, crushed

1 teaspoon dried basil, crushed

1 teaspoon freshly ground black pepper

1 London broil (3½ pounds)

Combine tomato juice, Worcestershire sauce, horseradish, sherry, and seasonings in a bowl. Spread the steak out in a single layer in a baking dish. Spoon tomato juice mixture over meat, spreading to cover. Turn meat to coat other side. Cover and refrigerate for at least 2 hours, or set aside at room temperature for 30 minutes.

Remove meat from marinade, and discard marinade. Grill steak over medium-high heat for 8 minutes. Turn and grill for 7 to 10 minutes longer for medium-rare, or until desired doneness.

Let steak rest at room temperature for approximately 5 minutes. Slice steak diagonally into thin strips before serving. ✸

CB'S TAILGATE CHEESE STEAKS

2 onions, thinly sliced

1 pound sirloin steak (you can also use lamb, pork, or chicken)

4 cups shredded cheddar, jack, or havarti cheese

Salt and pepper

4 hoagie rolls

4 sheets heavy-duty foil

Preheat grill to medium high. Spray foil with nonstick cooking spray, and place one-quarter of the onion slices on each sheet.

Cut meat into strips ⅛ inch thick; season with salt and pepper. Add one-quarter of the steak strips, followed by one-quarter of the cheese to the onions on each foil sheet. Fold foil over mixture, sealing edges firmly. Leave some space for food to expand during cooking.

Grill 10 minutes on covered grill, turning once. Serve on hoagie rolls, topped with favorite BBQ sauce. ✲

3

BEEF, LAMB & VEAL

This is a great preparation method for picnics, tailgating, or any time you have a large group of folks to serve. Prepare the foil packets in advance, keep cool, and place on the grill as you need them. —CB

"EAGLES" TAILGATING STEAK

⅓ cup Worcestershire sauce

¼ tablespoon dry red wine

¼ tablespoon red wine vinegar

½ tablespoon dark brown sugar

2 cloves garlic, minced

½ tablespoon steak sauce

1½ pound flank steak

[*Philadelphia Eagles fan and tailgater
Kevin Gibbons provided this easy recipe.*]

Combine first six ingredients in a bowl. Place steak in a plastic bag or container, and pour marinade over meat. Let marinate in refrigerator overnight.

Remove steaks from marinade; reserve marinade. Cook steak over hot grill, approximately 5 minutes per side. While steak is grilling, bring reserved marinade to a boil in a saucepan until mixture is reduced by one-third. Let steak rest 10 minutes.

Cut on the grain, and serve with sauce. ❊

3

BEEF, LAMB & VEAL

HICKORY BEEF RIBS

2 racks beef ribs (8–10 ribs each)

RIB MIXTURE

½ cup soy sauce
1 tablespoon steak spice
1 tablespoon garlic salt
1 tablespoon fresh garlic, chopped
1 teaspoon chili flakes

SAUCE

1 large onion, diced
1 tablespoon olive oil
3 28-ounce cans tomato
   sauce
1 19-ounce jar apple sauce
2 cups brown sugar
1 cup honey
½ cup soy sauce
½ cup white vinegar
4 tablespoons molasses
1¼ teaspoon liquid
   smoke
Salt and pepper

Fill a large pot with water, and add rib mixture. Bring water to a boil. Add ribs; boil for 1 hour.

Sauté diced onion in olive oil until soft. Add remaining ingredients to a large sauce pot; bring to a boil; then continue to simmer over medium heat for 30 minutes. Remove ribs from water, and pat dry with paper towels. Coat with enough sauce to cover; let stand 30 minutes. Grill ribs on medium-high for 8 to 10 minutes, basting and turning often to avoid burning. ✹

GREEK BEEF SALAD

1 pound top round steak, approximately
  1 inch thick

6 cups romaine lettuce

1 medium cucumber, thinly sliced

½ small red onion, cut into thin wedges

2 tablespoons crumbled feta cheese

8 Greek or black olives

2 pita breads, toasted, cut into wedges

MARINADE

⅔ cup fresh lemon juice

⅓ cup olive oil

½ teaspoon dried oregano

½ teaspoon salt and pepper

Whisk marinade ingredients in a small bowl. Place steak and one-half of marinade in plastic bag; turn to coat. Seal bag securely, and marinate in refrigerator 6 hours or overnight, turning occasionally. Refrigerate remaining half of marinade.

Remove steak; discard marinade. Place steak on medium-high grill, 12 to 15 minutes for medium rare, turning occasionally. Remove and let stand 10 minutes. Carve into thin slices. Combine sliced steak, lettuce, cucumber, and onion in a large bowl. Toss with reserved marinade mixture. Sprinkle with cheese and olives. Serve with pita wedges. ✸

4 Servings • Prep: 20 min. • Marinate: 2 hr. minimum • Grill: 15 min.

81

SIRLOIN, PASTA & ARTICHOKE SALAD WITH BALSAMIC VINAIGRETTE

1 pound boneless top sirloin steak,
   cut 1 inch thick

¼ cup tricolored fusilli or rotini
   pasta, cooked and drained

1 14-ounce can quartered artichoke hearts, drained

1 large red bell pepper, cut into thin strips

1 cup small, pitted, ripe olives

½ tablespoon fresh basil, chopped

1 cup prepared balsamic
   vinaigrette dressing

Place steak and ½ cup of dressing into a plastic bag; seal; and turn to coat. Marinate for 2 hours or overnight. Thirty minutes before cooking, remove steak from refrigerator. Remove from bag; discard marinade.

Cook steak on medium-high grill, 13 to 17 minutes, turning occasionally. Remove; let stand 10 minutes. Cut steak lengthwise in half; then slice crosswise thinly. Combine steak, pasta, artichoke hearts, bell pepper, olives, and basil in a large bowl. Add vinaigrette; toss. Serve immediately. ✿

3

BEEF, LAMB & VEAL

STEAK & ROASTED VEGETABLE SALAD

1 pound boneless beef top loin or
   tenderloin, cut 1 inch thick
8 cups torn salad greens
¾ cup prepared Italian dressing

Coat vegetables with vinegar, garlic, rosemary, salt, and pepper. Grill vegetables; then cool slightly.

Place steaks on grill for 8 to 11 minutes for medium-rare to medium doneness, turning occasionally. Remove; let stand 10 minutes.

Carve steaks and roughly chop vegetables; season with salt. Arrange beef and vegetables on greens. Serve with dressing. ✺

GRILLED VEGETABLES
2 portabella mushroom caps
1 large red, yellow, or green bell pepper, cut into
   1-inch-wide strips
1 medium Japanese eggplant, sliced lengthwise
   in ¼-inch slices
1 medium red onion, cut into ½-inch slices,
1 zucchini, sliced lengthwise in ¼-inch slices
½ tablespoon balsamic vinegar
½ large clove garlic, minced
1 teaspoon dried rosemary

JAPANESE BEEF STEAK SALAD WITH SESAME DRESSING

1 pound boneless top sirloin,
  cut 1 inch thick
3 cups each sliced Napa cabbage
  and romaine lettuce
½ cup each thinly-sliced carrot,
  cucumber and radish
1 cup hot cooked rice
24 pea pods, blanched

Prepare marinade by combining sherry, soy sauce, vinegar, hoisin sauce, and ginger in a small bowl. Place steak and ⅓ cup marinade in plastic bag. Close bag securely, and marinate in refrigerator 2 hours, turning once.

For dressing, add ¼ cup water, green onion, sugar, and sesame oil to remaining marinade; mix well. Remove steak; discard marinade. Place steak on medium-high grill, 13 to 17 minutes for medium-rare to medium doneness, turning occasionally. Let stand 5 minutes. Carve steak.

Combine cabbage, lettuce, carrot, and radishes; divide among 4 plates. Arrange cucumber, rice, pea pods, and steak on salads. Top with dressing. ✿

3

BEEF, LAMB & VEAL

MARINADE AND DRESSING
3 tablespoons each dry sherry,
  reduced-sodium soy sauce,
  and rice wine vinegar
2 tablespoons hoisin sauce
½ teaspoon grated fresh ginger
2 tablespoons green onion, chopped
1 tablespoon each sugar and
  dark sesame oil

ASIAN STEAK
IN LETTUCE WRAPS

6–8 Servings • Prep: 30 min. • Marinate: 30 min. • Grill: 5–10 min.

85

¾ cup soy sauce

¼ cup rice vinegar

2½ tablespoons sugar

2 tablespoons fresh ginger, minced

1 tablespoon Asian sesame oil

1 teaspoon Asian chili paste

3 garlic cloves, minced

2 scallions, chopped

1 flank steak, approximately 1½ pounds

1 ripe mango, peeled and julienned

1 small red onion, julienned

3 tablespoons lime juice

24 lettuce leaves (Bibb or romaine)

2 tablespoons toasted sesame seeds

[*This recipe can also be prepared using chicken, shrimp, or pork.*]

Combine first eight marinade ingredients in a bowl. Reserve approximately one-quarter of the marinade. Place the steak in a plastic bag, and pour the larger portion of marinade over it. Seal the bag tightly, and turn to distribute the marinade. Let rest at room temperature for 30 minutes.

Remove steak from marinade, and grill over high heat for approximately 2 to 4 minutes per side, until seared on the surface but still pink at the center. Let steak rest for 5 minutes.

Meanwhile, combine the mango, onion, and lime juice in a bowl. Slice the steak across the grain into very thin strips approximately ¼ inch thick. Cut the strips into thirds. Coat the steak with the reserved marinade, and arrange on a platter. Surround with a plate of lettuce leaves, the mango mixture, and the sesame seeds. To assemble, allow guests to spoon some strips of the steak onto each lettuce leaf, topping with mango mixture and sprinkling with sesame seeds. ❀

3

BEEF, LAMB & VEAL

CHAMPION SMOKED BEEF BRISKET

1 beef brisket (10 to 12 pounds)
16 ounces beer
1 orange, thinly sliced
1 lemon, thinly sliced

Combine rub ingredients, and massage into brisket. Seal meat in a plastic bag, and refrigerate overnight.

Remove brisket from the refrigerator, and let stand at room temperature for 1 hour before grilling. Prepare a smoker, and bring temperature to 220°F. Fill water pan with hot water and 16 ounces of beer. Float orange and lemon in pan. Combine basting ingredients, and pour into clean, empty spray bottle.

Place brisket in center of grill over water pan, fat side up. Loosely place bacon on top of brisket. Cook brisket 1 to 1½ hours per pound, for a minimum of 12 hours, basting every hour with brisket spray. Brisket is done when internal temperature reaches 150°F. Meat will shrink dramatically and turn almost black. Remove meat from grill; spray once more; and let rest, sealed in aluminum foil. Slice across the grain, and serve with your favorite barbecue sauce. ❂

BRISKET RUB

½ cup paprika
¼ cup black pepper
¼ cup salt
¼ cup turbinado or brown sugar
2 tablespoons chili powder
1 tablespoon onion powder
1 tablespoon dry mustard
1 tablespoon celery salt
1 teaspoon red pepper

BRISKET BASTING SPRAY

1 cup apple cider vinegar
1 can beer
1 tablespoon Worcestershire sauce
1 tablespoon olive oil
1 pound thinly sliced bacon

8–10 Servings • Prep: 15 min. • Marinate: overnight • Grill: 1 hr. per lb.

87

CB'S TEXAS-STYLE SMOKED BRISKET

1 beef brisket (5 to 7 pounds), trimmed except for layer of fat on one side

2 cups CB's BBQ dry rub mixture (Recipe below.)

1 cup CB's BBQ sauce (Recipe below.)

12 ounces pilsner beer

12 ounces apple cider vinegar

[*This recipe uses traditional barbecue methods of indirect low heat of approximately 225°F–250°F degrees. —CB*]

One day before cooking, rub brisket with dry rub mixture, and wrap meat in plastic wrap. Refrigerate overnight.

Two hours before cooking, remove brisket from the refrigerator. Prepare smoker or barbecue for indirect heat.

When smoke and heat reach desired level, unwrap brisket and place fat side up in the center of the grill. Place an aluminum pan filled with 1 inch of water underneath the meat to catch drips. Insert an ovenproof meat thermometer covered with plastic wrap or foil into the meat. Close lid, and let smoke at least 2 hours. Add wood chips and charcoal as necessary to maintain consistent heat.

At 2 hours and every hour thereafter, mop brisket with BBQ sauce. When meat reaches an internal temperature approximately 10 degrees short of desired doneness (160°F–180°F), remove; cover with foil; and wrap in kitchen towels. Allow to rest for 30 minutes. Internal temperature will continue to rise about 10 more degrees. Slice and serve. ❁

3

BEEF, LAMB & VEAL

CB'S BBQ DRY RUB

2 parts Kosher salt

1 part freshly ground black pepper

1 part dry mustard

1 part chili powder

CB'S TOMATO BBQ SAUCE

2 parts tomato ketchup

1 part dark brown sugar

1 part balsamic or apple cider vinegar

SMOKED RIB ROAST

1 medium onion, diced

1 bay leaf

Sprig each of fresh thyme,
 marjoram, and oregano

2 tablespoons oil

2 cloves garlic, finely chopped

2 cups red wine

3-pound boneless cross rib roast

[*Enjoy with roasted potatoes, gravy, horseradish, and Yorkshire pudding, or slice for sandwiches the next day.*]

Combine onion, bay leaf, herbs, oil, garlic, and red wine to make marinade. Trim excess fat from the meat. Place roast in a large plastic bag or airtight container, and pour in the marinade. Seal bag tightly, and turn gently to distribute the marinade. Refrigerate overnight, turning occasionally.

Remove roast from marinade, and pat dry with paper towels. Preheat smoker to 220°F. Place roast on the upper grate of the smoker. Using your favorite flavored wood chips, smoke the roast for 7 to 8 hours or until internal temperature reaches 150°F. Let rest 10 minutes before carving. ✸

PITA POCKET LAMB BURGERS WITH SPINACH & FETA

1 tablespoon unsalted butter

1 10-ounce package frozen spinach, thawed

1 teaspoon minced garlic

1 teaspoon chopped fresh oregano

1¼ cups crumbled feta cheese

2 tablespoons cottage cheese

2 pounds ground lamb

1½ teaspoons minced garlic

1 tablespoon chopped parsley

½ teaspoon sweet paprika

1 teaspoon freshly ground black pepper

4 pita pockets

1 lemon

Melt butter in a saucepan over medium heat. Add the spinach, garlic, and oregano. Cook, stirring constantly, until all the liquid evaporates, approximately 4 minutes. Keep warm.

Combine lamb with next four ingredients. Mix well, and form four patties approximately ¾ inch thick. Grill the burgers over medium-high heat, 4½ minutes per side for medium-rare, or until desired doneness.

Cut lemon in half, and squeeze juice over the burgers a few minutes before removing them from grill. Place a dollop of the spinach mixture on top of each burger; then place burgers inside pita pockets. ✺

HERB-CRUSTED LAMB CHOPS

2 teaspoons fresh thyme

2 teaspoons fresh mint

2 teaspoons fresh rosemary

1 teaspoons fresh crushed garlic

1 teaspoon dried or fresh oregano

1 teaspoon steak spice

6–8 shoulder or baby lamb chops

Mix first six ingredients in small, flat dish. Place chops in marinade. Marinate for 1 hour. Grill over medium heat 6 to 8 minutes for medium doneness, turning frequently to avoid burning. ❁

BABY LAMB CHOPS WITH COUSCOUS

1 cup chicken stock

½ cup couscous, uncooked

¼ cup tomato, chopped and seeded

1 green onion, chopped

2 tablespoons parsley, chopped

2 tablespoons red wine vinegar

6 tablespoons olive oil

Salt and pepper to taste

1 sprig fresh rosemary,
   chopped

8 baby lamb chops or
   4 shoulder lamb chops

In a saucepan, bring chicken stock to a boil; stir in couscous. Simmer 5 minutes; remove from heat. Let stand, covered, for 20 minutes. Spoon into serving bowl. Chill for one hour.

Stir couscous, and add tomato, green onion, parsley, vinegar, 3 tablespoons olive oil, salt, and pepper. Mix well. Place in microwaveable bowl, and warm 1 minute in microwave until heated through.

Preheat the grill, and oil the grill grates. Rub lamb with additional olive oil; sprinkle with rosemary and pepper. Grill chops for 5 minutes on each side. Serve with warm couscous. ❁

3

BEEF, LAMB & VEAL

ROTISSERIE-ROASTED LEG OF LAMB

4-pound boneless leg of lamb

4 cloves of garlic, peeled and cut into slivers

3 tablespoons dried oregano

3 tablespoons dried rosemary

1 teaspoon dried thyme

5 tablespoons olive oil

Salt and freshly ground black pepper

Olive oil for basting

Juice of 2 lemons

Using a knife, create six to eight deep slashes at various points in roast, and insert garlic pieces. Combine the herbs, oil, salt, and pepper, and rub the meat with the seasonings. Allow meat to rest for 20 minutes.

Preheat the grill. Insert spit rod lengthwise through center of the lamb; secure with holding forks on each side.

Grill for 45 minutes to 1 hour, basting lamb with olive oil and lemon juice every 10 to 15 minutes. Allow the lamb to rest for 20 minutes; then carve and serve. ✸

GOLDEN HEART LAMB

1 boneless shoulder roast of lamb,
(3 to 4 pounds)

Salt and pepper to taste

12 ounces dried apricots

1 12-ounce bottle creamy Italian
salad dressing

2 tablespoons minced
garlic

[*Hal Walker, a member of the Hasty-Bake Ole Smokers team of Kansas City, Kansas, has won several awards at the American Royal Barbecue Contest and the Great Lenexa, Kansas Barbecue Battle with this recipe.*]

Remove lamb from roasting net, or untie twine. Unroll meat, and trim off fat; sprinkle meat liberally with salt and pepper. Stuff lamb with apricots. Fold and re-tie lamb securely. Place in sealable plastic bag. Pour mixture of salad dressing and garlic over lamb; seal bag. Marinate in refrigerator for 12 hours or longer.

Drain, reserving marinade. Sear lamb over hot grill for 5 minutes per side. Grill over low heat for 1½ hours or until done to taste, basting with reserved marinade during first hour. Remove to serving platter; cut into thin slices. ✳

GRILLED SAGE VEAL CHOPS

4 veal chops (6 to 8 ounces each)
2 tablespoons olive oil
16 fresh sage leaves
White pepper and salt to taste

Brush chops evenly on both sides with olive oil. Season with salt and pepper to taste. Press 2 sage leaves on each side of the chops, and marinate in refrigerator for at least one hour.

Grill over high heat for approximately 5 to 6 minutes on each side. ❊

CB'S VEAL CHOP FORESTIER

1 12–14 ounce veal chop,
approximately 1 inch thick, or
2 smaller chops

2 teaspoons olive oil

3 tablespoons unsalted butter

4 tablespoons rough-chopped
shallots

1 teaspoon chopped garlic

2 tablespoons red port

2 tablespoons brandy or cognac

3 ounces Chanterelle mushrooms,
cut into bite-size pieces

Salt and pepper to taste

½ teaspoon flour (optional)

Allow veal chop to rest at room temperature for at least 20 minutes before cooking. Preheat grill to high. Season veal with salt and pepper, and brush lightly with oil or butter.

Reduce grill heat to medium. Place chop on hot section of grates, and turn down flames underneath meat. Sear for approximately 4 to 5 minutes; then turn and place on new section of hot grill, turning flame off beneath chop and relighting other side of grill. Sear for just a few minutes on this side.

Remove chop; allow to rest approximately 10 minutes before serving. ❁

FORESTIER SAUCE

Heat butter in sauté pan on medium until it begins to bubble. Add shallots, browning slightly; then add garlic, making sure mixture doesn't burn. Add mushrooms, stirring to coat in mixture. When mushrooms begin to brown, stir in port. Let mixture reduce slightly before adding brandy. Stir in flour, and allow sauce to continue cooking for 3 to 5 minutes. Ladle over chop. Sprinkle with chopped parsley.

4 Pork

(Left) *Beer-Basted Baby Back Ribs, page 107*

GARLIC & ORANGE-MARINATED GRILLED PORK CHOPS

4 pork chops, boneless or bone-in,
   about 1¼ inches thick
½ cup orange juice
½ tablespoon olive oil
½ crushed garlic cloves
½ teaspoon ground cumin
¼ teaspoon coarsely ground
   black pepper

4

PORK

[*Enjoy the taste of the West Coast with these California-inspired marinated chops.*]

Place chops in large, self-sealing plastic bag. Combine remaining ingredients in small bowl, and pour over chops. Seal bag, and refrigerate 4 to 24 hours. Preheat grill to medium. Remove chops from marinade (discarding marinade), and grill 12 to 15 minutes, turning to brown evenly. Serve chops immediately. ❁

SPIT-ROASTED PORK CHOPS

2 tablespoons olive oil

8 center-cut pork chops,
 ¾-inch-thick

BBQ RUB
¼ cup kosher salt

¼ cup paprika

½ teaspoon cayenne pepper

⅓ cup brown sugar

1 tablespoon garlic powder

2 teaspoons celery salt

GLAZE
¼ cup fresh lime juice

½ cup honey

2 teaspoons dried thyme

Pinch of cayenne

⅛ teaspoon ground cumin

¼ cup fresh cilantro leaves,
 chopped

2 limes, each cut
 into 8 wedges

Pour olive oil into shallow dish, and mix with barbecue rub ingredients. Dip chops into spice mixture, turning to coat evenly. Preheat grill to medium-high. Coat rotisserie basket with nonstick cooking spray; lay chops in basket; and close lid tightly. Load basket onto spit rod.

Combine glaze ingredients. When chops have cooked for 10 minutes, stop rotisserie and baste chops with glaze. Restart rotisserie, and continue to grill chops another 25 minutes or until thickest part reaches 160°F, stopping rotisserie three more times to baste. Remove chops from basket; garnish with cilantro and lime wedges. Serve. ❁

DRUNKEN PORK CHOPS

2 cups dry red wine

5 bay leaves

2 tablespoons fresh
rosemary, minced

1½ teaspoons ground
coriander

½ teaspoon nutmeg

½ teaspoon ground cloves

6 pork chops,
1½-inches-thick

Salt and pepper to taste

Olive oil for grilling

[*Simple and delicious, these chops can be made for a backyard dinner with friends. Serve with a mixed green salad followed by fresh fruits and cheese.*]

Combine red wine, bay leaves, rosemary, coriander, nutmeg, and cloves in a glass dish. Place chops in marinade mixture. Marinate overnight in refrigerator, turning occasionally.

Drain chops, and pat dry; discard used marinade. Season with salt and pepper, and lightly brush with olive oil. Preheat grill to medium-high. Grill chops 6 to 8 minutes on each side. ✺

4

PORK

SMOKED PORK CHOPS WITH POLENTA & CRANBERRY CHUTNEY

6 cups water

1 pound coarse-ground cornmeal

2 teaspoons salt

1 cup Parmesan cheese, grated

5 tablespoons butter

12 ounces spinach

12-ounce pork chops, cured and smoked

Cranberry Chutney (recipe follows)

CRANBERRY CHUTNEY

Saute 1 chopped onion in 1 tablespoon oil; stir in 2 cups fresh cranberries, 1 cup water, and ¾ cup sugar. Boil 1 minute; stir in 2 tablespoons dry mustard and ⅛ teaspoon each ground cloves, cinnamon, and mace.

In a heavy, large saucepan, whisk together 6 cups water, cornmeal, and salt; bring to a boil; then reduce heat to low and simmer, stirring often, for 5 to 8 minutes or until polenta becomes thick, soft, and creamy. Stir in Parmesan and 4 tablespoons butter. Cover, and keep warm.

In a medium pan, saute spinach in 1 tablespoon butter for 3 to 4 minutes until softened. Set aside. Grill chops over medium-high heat about 10 minutes, turning once. Serve with spinach, polenta, and cranberry chutney. ⊛

[*Because the chops are already smoked and need just a few minutes on the grill, prepare the other ingredients in this recipe first. The cranberry chutney can be made a day in advance.*]

KANSAS CITY MOP RIBS

6 to 8 pounds pork spare ribs, long ends only

KANSAS CITY-STYLE BARBECUE SAUCE

(1½ cups)

1 small onion, chopped

2 cloves garlic, minced

1 tablespoon vegetable oil

1 cup ketchup

⅓ cup molasses

¼ cup distilled white vinegar

2 tablespoons chili powder

2 teaspoons dry mustard

1 teaspoon celery salt

1 teaspoon paprika

1 teaspoon ground cayenne chili

½ teaspoon freshly ground black pepper

¼ cup water or more if needed

Sauté onion and garlic in oil until onions
are soft. Add remaining ingredients; simmer
for 30 minutes or until thickened.

KANSAS CITY DRY RUB

(⅔ cup)

2 tablespoons brown sugar

2 tablespoons ground paprika

1 tablespoon white sugar

1 tablespoon garlic salt

1 tablespoon celery salt

1 tablespoon chili powder

2 teaspoons freshly ground black pepper

1 teaspoon ground cayenne chili

½ teaspoon dry mustard

Combine all ingredients in a bowl,
and mix well. Store any
unused rub in sealed
container in freezer.

Sprinkle rub evenly over ribs, and let marinate for 2 hours at room temperature or overnight in refrigerator. Prepare smoker, and place ribs on grates. Smoke at approximately 200°F for 4 hours. Baste frequently with sauce during last 30 minutes of smoking. Serve with additional sauce on the side. ✺

ASIAN-STYLE BABY BACK RIBS

2 racks baby backs or other favorite ribs

ASIAN BARBECUE SAUCE

(3 cups)

6 cloves garlic, minced

2 tablespoons ginger, finely minced

8 serrano peppers, minced, including seeds

4 small green onions, green and white parts, minced

¼ cup cilantro, minced

1 tablespoon lime zest, grated

Juice from 3 limes

1 cup hoisin sauce

½ cup wine vinegar

¼ cup Thai fish sauce

¼ cup honey

2 tablespoons soy sauce

2 tablespoons canola oil

To make sauce, stir all ingredients together except ribs. Coat ribs evenly on both sides with one-half of the sauce. Reserve remaining sauce to serve with ribs. Marinate ribs, refrigerated, for at least 1 hour. For more flavor, marinate overnight.

Preheat grill to medium (325°F), and oil grill grates. Baste ribs occasionally with marinade during cooking, stopping 15 minutes before removing ribs from grill.

To serve, cut each side of ribs in half, or into individual ribs. Serve immediately with remaining sauce. ✵

BEER-BASTED BABY BACK RIBS

6 cups beer

2½ cups brown sugar

1½ cups apple cider vinegar

1½ tablespoons chili powder

1½ tablespoons ground cumin

1 tablespoon dry mustard

2 teaspoons salt

2 teaspoons dried crushed
   red pepper

2 bay leaves

8 pounds baby back pork
   ribs, cut into 4-rib sections

Bring first nine ingredients to a boil in a large pot. Reduce heat, and simmer about 1 minute to blend flavors. Add half of ribs to sauce. Cover pot, and simmer until ribs are tender, turning frequently, about 25 minutes. Transfer ribs to baking dish. Repeat with remaining ribs. Boil barbecue sauce until reduced to 3 cups, about 40 minutes. Discard bay leaves. (Can be prepared 1 day ahead. Cover ribs and sauce separately, and refrigerate. Warm sauce before continuing.)

Preheat grill to medium, and oil the grill grates. Brush ribs with some of sauce; sprinkle with salt. Grill ribs until heated through, browned, and well-glazed, brushing occasionally with sauce, about 6 minutes per side. ❋

4

PORK

MUSTARD-BOURBON BABY BACK RIBS

3 racks baby back ribs
  (4 to 6 pounds)

SPICE RUB

2 tablespoons ground cumin

1 tablespoon chili powder

1 tablespoon dry mustard

1 tablespoon coarse salt

1½ teaspoons cayenne pepper

1½ teaspoons ground cardamom

1½ teaspoons ground cinnamon

Mix ingredients in medium bowl.

Rub spice mixture over both sides of rib racks. Arrange ribs on a large baking sheet. Cover, and refrigerate overnight. Preheat grill to medium, and oil grill grates. Cut rib racks into four to six rib sections, and arrange on cooking grate. Grill until meat is tender, turning occasionally, for about 40 minutes. Cut rib sections between bones into individual ribs, and lay flat in baking dish. Transfer 3 cups sauce to small bowl; place remaining sauce in small saucepan; and reserve. Brush ribs with sauce from bowl. Return ribs to grill. Place pan of reserved sauce at edge of grill to warm. Grill ribs until brown and crisp on edges, brushing with more sauce from bowl and turning occasionally, about 10 minutes.

Serve ribs with warm sauce. ✿

SAUCE

1 tablespoon vegetable oil

2 bunches scallions, chopped

2 cups white onions, chopped

8 garlic cloves, chopped

2 cups brown sugar

1 cup ketchup

1 cup tomato paste

1 cup Dijon mustard

1 cup water

½ cup Worcestershire sauce

½ cup apple-cider vinegar

½ cup apple juice

1 large dried ancho chili, stemmed,
  seeded, and cut into small pieces

1 tablespoon ground cumin

1½ cups bourbon

Salt and pepper, to taste

Heat oil in large pot over medium-low heat. Add scallions, onions, and garlic; sauté until tender. Mix in remaining ingredients, adding bourbon last. Simmer sauce, stirring occasionally, until reduced to 7 cups, about 1 hour. Season to taste with salt and pepper. Refrigerate in covered container for up to 2 weeks.

"MEMPHIS IN MAY" RIBS

3 racks baby back ribs
   (4 to 6 pounds)
1 cup Memphis Rib Rub
1 cup Memphis-Style Finishing
   Sauce

MEMPHIS RIB RUB

¼ cup paprika
2 tablespoons garlic salt
1 tablespoon freshly ground
   black pepper
2 tablespoons brown sugar
1 tablespoon onion powder
1 tablespoon dried oregano
1 tablespoon dry mustard
1½ teaspoons ground cayenne

Combine all ingredients in
bowl, and mix well. Freeze any
unused rub in sealed container.

FINISHING SAUCE

1 cup tomato sauce
1 cup red wine vinegar
2 teaspoon Louisiana-style hot sauce
1 tablespoon butter
½ teaspoon freshly ground black pepper
½ teaspoon salt
½ cup beer

Place all ingredients in saucepan, and
bring to a boil, stirring constantly.
Reduce heat and simmer, uncovered,
for 15 minutes. Serve warm with ribs.

In a shallow dish, pour rub over
ribs, massaging into both sides.
Cover, and refrigerate for 4 to 6
hours. Remove ribs from refrigerator, and bring to room temperature. Preheat grill to 300°F
to 350°F, and oil grill grates.
Grill ribs, covered, for 1 hour,
turning often. Continue cooking for 30 minutes, basting with
finishing sauce. (If smoking
ribs, maintain smoke at 200°F
to 220°F, and smoke for 2 hours.
Brush sauce over ribs several
times during last hour of smoking, turning ribs occasionally.)
Remove ribs from grill, and
serve with sauce. ✷

4

PORK

*This recipe was a recent
finalist in the annual
Memphis in May World
Championship Barbecue
Cooking Contest.*

MONTREAL JERK RIBS

2 racks baby back ribs

Rub dry ingredients onto all surfaces of ribs. Grill ribs over indirect heat about 1½ hours in covered grill, turning occasionally, until ribs are very tender. (Or roast ribs on rack in shallow pan in 350°F oven for 1½ hours.) Cut into one- or two-rib portions to serve. ✸

MONTREAL JERK RUB

2 tablespoons dried minced
  onions
1 tablespoon onion powder
4 teaspoons ground thyme
2 teaspoons salt
2 teaspoons ground allspice
½ teaspoon ground nutmeg
½ teaspoon ground cinnamon
1 tablespoon sugar
2 teaspoons black pepper
1 teaspoon cayenne

In a small jar with a tight-
fitting lid, shake together all
dry ingredients until blended.

TOMATO-BASIL RIBS WITH ZESTY RANCH DRESSING

6 boneless country-style pork ribs

½ cup margarine, softened

1 medium tomato, halved and thinly sliced

1 1-ounce package basil leaves

¼ teaspoon salt or to taste

⅛ teaspoon black pepper or to taste

1 cup ranch-style dressing

½ teaspoon hot pepper sauce

Butcher's twine

[*Lance Hensley of Montgomery, Alabama, created this first-place recipe for stuffed, country-style ribs for the Alabama National Fair.*]

Preheat grill to medium-high. Slice each rib down center lengthwise, cutting halfway through. Spread equal amounts of margarine down center of each rib. Arrange tomato slices and basil leaves down center of each. Wrap each rib with butcher's twine in several places to hold rib together. Sprinkle evenly with salt and pepper.

Grill ribs 15 to 18 minutes or until no longer pink in center, turning frequently using spatula or tongs to handle easily. Watch closely for flare-ups. Margarine will melt and flames will occur. Move pieces to another area of grill when this happens. Combine salad dressing and hot pepper sauce in small bowl, and stir until well blended. Serve as dip for ribs. ✲

SPICY THAI PORK KABOBS

1 large onion, chopped

1 clove garlic, minced

⅓ cup creamy peanut butter

3 tablespoons soy sauce

1½ tablespoons lemon juice

2 tablespoons brown sugar

1 teaspoon ground coriander

¼ cup chili sauce

1 teaspoon salt

1 teaspoon ground cumin

½ teaspoon red pepper

½ teaspoon freshly ground pepper

2 pounds pork tenderloin, cut into
   1½-inch cubes

Combine all ingredients except pork in blender, and blend well. Place pork into a sealable plastic bag; pour mixture over pork. Refrigerate about 6 hours. Preheat grill to medium. Thread pork on skewers, and grill about 20 minutes, turning frequently. ❂

HONEY PORK TENDERLOIN KABOBS

1½ cup bourbon (or 2 tablespoons
    cider vinegar)
½ cup honey
½ cup mustard
1 teaspoon dried tarragon
3 to 4 yams or sweet potatoes, cut
    into 24 1-inch cubes
1½ pound pork tenderloin, cut into
    24 1-inch cubes
4 ripe unpeeled peaches, pitted
    and quartered
4 green peppers, each cut into 8
    2-inch pieces
8 yellow onions, each cut into 4
    2-inch pieces
Olive oil for grilling

Mix first four ingredients in a bowl; stir well; and set aside. Steam or boil sweet potatoes until crisp-tender. Alternately thread sweet potato cubes, pork cubes, peach quarters, green pepper pieces, and onion pieces onto each of eight 10-inch skewers. Brush kabobs with honey mixture. Preheat grill to medium, and lightly oil grilling surface. Grill 5 minutes on each side, basting occasionally. ❀

ASIAN SESAME TENDERLOIN

2 pork tenderloins, about ¾ to 1 pound each

MARINADE

6 tablespoons soy sauce

1 small onion, finely chopped

¼ cup brown sugar

2 tablespoons vegetable oil

2 tablespoons sesame oil

3 tablespoons water

2 cloves garlic, peeled and minced

2 teaspoons ground ginger

½ teaspoon black pepper

⅛ teaspoon cayenne pepper

1½ tablespoons sesame seeds

Mix marinade ingredients in a bowl. Trim any excess fat and skin from tenderloins. Pour marinade over tenderloins in large plastic storage bag or nonmetallic dish. Seal bag or cover dish with plastic wrap. Refrigerate for at least 6 hours or overnight, turning occasionally.

Preheat grill to medium-high. Remove tenderloins from marinade; discard marinade. Place tenderloins on cooking grate over indirect heat. Close lid, and grill for 10 to 15 minutes. Turn tenderloins; close the lid; and grill for 10 to 15 minutes more. Pork is considered done when internal temperature reaches 155°F and center is barely pink. ✸

4 Servings • Prep: 45 min. • Marinate: 2 hr. • Grill: 15–20 min.

117

CHIPOTLE CHILI PORK TENDERLOIN

5 canned chipotle chilies in adobo,
  stemmed, plus 2 tablespoons
  of sauce from can
5 garlic cloves, thinly sliced
1 strip of orange zest
¾ cup fresh orange juice
¼ cup lime juice
2 tablespoons red wine vinegar
1 tablespoon tomato paste
1 teaspoon dried oregano
1 teaspoon ground cumin
½ teaspoon freshly ground pepper
1½ pounds pork tenderloin

In saucepan, combine chipotles and their sauce with garlic, orange zest, orange juice, lime juice, red wine vinegar, tomato paste, oregano, cumin, and pepper. Simmer over high heat until reduced by one-third, about 3 minutes. Transfer sauce to food processor, and puree until smooth. Allow marinade to cool.

Trim any excess fat and skin from the tenderloin. Coat pork with ¼ cup of marinade, and refrigerate for 2 hours. Preheat grill to high. Grill pork, turning until cooked through, about 15 minutes. Pork is done when internal temperature reaches 155°F and center is barely pink. Let stand for 10 minutes before slicing and serving. ✺

4

PORK

PANCETTA-WRAPPED TENDERLOIN

2 pork tenderloins, about 1 pound each
¼ pound pancetta (Italian-style bacon), thinly sliced
Cotton string

RUB
1 tablespoon garlic, minced
2 teaspoons fresh rosemary, minced
2 teaspoons kosher salt
¼ teaspoon freshly ground black pepper

In a small bowl, combine rub ingredients. Trim any excess fat and skin from tenderloins, and spread them evenly with rub, pressing spices into the meat. Cut six 12-inch pieces of cotton string, three for each tenderloin. Wrap tenderloins with slices of pancetta, and secure pancetta with string. Allow to rest at room temperature for 20 to 30 minutes before grilling.

Preheat grill to medium. Grill tenderloins over indirect heat about 25 to 30 minutes, turning once halfway through grilling time. Pork is done when internal temperature reaches 155°F and center is barely pink. Move tenderloins over to direct medium heat for last 3 minutes to crisp pancetta. Allow meat to rest for 10 minutes; then snip strings with scissors, and remove them. Cut tenderloins in thin slices on bias, and serve warm. ✹

4 Servings • Prep: 45 min. • Marinate: 8 hr.–overnight • Grill: 60 min.

PESTO TENDERLOIN ON A PLANK

2 pounds pork tenderloin

1 plank (hickory, alder, or oak), soaked in water

Pesto recipe (See below.)

GARLIC-SAGE PESTO

20 fresh sage leaves

4 large cloves garlic, chopped

Zest of 1 lemon

2 teaspoons salt

1 tablespoon olive oil

SUN-DRIED TOMATO PESTO

1½ cups sun-dried tomatoes, packed in oil, drained

6 garlic cloves, peeled

1 cup Parmesan cheese, grated

1 cup fresh basil leaves

½ cup olive oil

2 tablespoons balsamic vinegar

PARMESAN-BASIL PESTO

1⅓ cups basil leaves

1½ teaspoons garlic, chopped

¼ cup pine nuts, toasted

½ cup Parmesan cheese, grated

¼ cup olive oil

Salt and pepper to taste

In food processor, blend pesto ingredients for one of the pestos until smooth. Trim any excess fat and skin from tenderloin. Spread pesto over entire pork tenderloin, and seal in plastic storage bag. Marinate at least 8 hours or overnight in refrigerator.

Let stand at room temperature for about 15 minutes before grilling. Place marinated pork loin on prepared plank. Preheat grill to medium-high. Grill tenderloin for about 1 hour. Pork is done when internal temperature reaches 155°F and center is barely pink. ✸

4 Servings • Prep: 20 min. • Marinate: 30 min. minimum • Grill: 15–20 min.

121

TERIYAKI PORK TENDERLOIN

1 fresh garlic clove

4 to 5 sprigs fresh rosemary

1½ cups teriyaki marinade

2½ to 3 pounds pork tenderloin

[*Try this with roasted-garlic mashed potatoes and grilled vegetables.*]

Chop garlic clove and fresh rosemary; then add them to the teriyaki. Trim any excess fat and skin from tenderloin. Add tenderloin to marinade, and allow to marinate for at least 30 minutes. (Tenderloin is better when marinated longer.) Preheat grill to high, and turn it down to medium-high just before cooking. Sear meat on both sides. After about 10 to 15 minutes of cooking, move tenderloin away from heat, and continue to cook over indirect heat for remaining time. Remove from grill, and let rest for 10 minutes. Slice tenderloin into medallions. Pork is done when internal temperature reaches 155°F and center is barely pink. ✹

4

PORK

GARLIC-LIME PORK TENDERLOIN

6 cloves garlic, chopped

2 tablespoons soy sauce

2 tablespoons fresh ginger, grated

2 tablespoons Dijon mustard

⅓ cup fresh lime juice

½ cup olive oil

⅛ teaspoon cayenne or to taste

6 pork tenderloin steaks

Blend first seven ingredients with salt and pepper to taste in blender or food processor. Trim any excess fat and skin from tenderloins. Combine steaks with marinade in large plastic storage bag. Seal bag, and marinate in refrigerator, turning occasionally, at least 1 day and up to 2 days. Preheat grill to medium-high. Remove steaks from refrigerator, and let stand at room temperature about 30 minutes. Remove steaks from marinade, and grill 15 to 20 minutes, turning every 5 minutes. Pork is done when internal temperature reaches 155°F and center is barely pink. ✸

MEDITERRANEAN GRILLED PORK ROAST

4-pound boneless pork loin roast

Zest of 2 lemons

5 garlic cloves, peeled

⅓ cup fresh rosemary leaves

¼ cup fresh sage leaves

¼ cup coarsely ground black pepper

Salt to taste

Pat pork roast dry. In bowl of food processor, place remaining six ingredients and process until fairly smooth. Pat seasoning mixture over all surfaces of roast. Place roast on medium-hot grill over indirect heat. Close grill lid, and grill for about 1 to 1¼ hours or until internal temperature reaches about 155°F. Remove pork from grill, and let rest about 10 minutes before slicing to serve. ✹

GREEK PORK LOIN ROAST

3 pounds boneless pork tenderloin

1 cup plain yogurt

1 cucumber, peeled and chopped

½ teaspoon garlic, crushed

½ teaspoon coriander seeds, crushed

¼ cup red onion, minced

¼ teaspoon crushed red pepper

Trim any excess fat and skin from tenderloin. Place pork tenderloin in large plastic storage bag. Pour marinade over tenderloin in bag. Seal bag, and marinate in refrigerator overnight. Remove from marinade; discard marinade.

Preheat grill to medium-high. Combine remaining six ingredients in a bowl; cover and refrigerate until ready to serve with pork roast. Place drip pan in grill under tenderloin. Grill 1 to 1½ hours over indirect heat in covered grill. Pork is done when internal temperature reaches 155°F and center is barely pink. Let meat rest 10 minutes before slicing thinly. ✹

MARINADE

¼ cup olive oil

¼ cup lemon juice

1 teaspoon oregano

1 teaspoon salt

1 teaspoon pepper

6 cloves garlic, minced

Combine the ingredients in a bowl.

SPIT-ROASTED PORK LOIN WITH ORANGE & MADEIRA SAUCE

1 pork tenderloin,
   3 to 4 pounds
Wood chips, soaked
   (optional)

MARINADE

½ cup Madeira wine
¼ cup honey
½ cup orange juice
¼ cup soy sauce
2 tablespoons orange
   zest, finely chopped
2 garlic cloves, minced
1 tablespoon fresh
   sage, or 1 teaspoon
   dried sage

Combine marinade ingredients, stirring well to dissolve honey. Trim any excess fat and skin from tenderloin. Add pork to marinade; cover; and let marinate for at least 4 hours or overnight in refrigerator. Bring to room temperature before cooking.

Preheat grill to medium-high. Add soaked wood chips for more flavor. Thread tenderloin on spit rod and place over grill. Roast about 1 to 1¼ hours. Pork is done when internal temperature reaches 155°F and center is barely pink. Transfer to warm platter, and cover with foil. Allow to rest for 10 minutes before slicing. Tenderloin can be served warm or cold.

Variation: To use this marinade recipe on pork chops, coat two (½ pound) bone-in pork loin chops with ¼ cup of marinade, and refrigerate for at least 2 hours or up to overnight. Grill over medium-high heat for about 5 minutes per side. ❁

4

PORK

GRILLED PORK BURGERS WITH APRICOT MAYONNAISE

1½ pounds lean ground pork

¼ cup minced onion

4 tablespoons cilantro, finely chopped

½ teaspoon seasoned salt

¼ cup mayonnaise

¼ cup apricot preserves

1 teaspoon lemon juice

2 teaspoons fresh cilantro, minced

12 slices Italian bread

[*This tangy-sweet mayonnaise also makes a delicious spread for cold pork-roast sandwiches.*]

In a large bowl, combine pork with onion, 4 tablespoons of cilantro, and seasoned salt; form into six patties, and set aside.

Preheat grill to medium-high. Combine mayonnaise, preserves, lemon juice, and 2 teaspoons of cilantro; set aside, or cover and refrigerate until ready to serve.

Grill burgers for about 5 to 6 minutes per side; remove and keep warm until an instant-read thermometer reads 160°F. Grill bread for 1 to 2 minutes per side until lightly toasted. To assemble sand-wiches, spread mayonnaise mixture on one side of each slice of bread. Top with burgers and remaining bread sliced at an angle over burger. Pass around any remaining apricot mayonnaise. ⊛

MA LANEY'S BARBECUE STEW

4 to 5 pounds smoked chicken

3 to 4 pounds barbecued Boston butt

2 large onions, chopped

3 cups chicken broth

2 12-ounce cans cream-style corn

2 12-ounce cans whole-kernel corn

1 12-ounce can baby lima beans

4 16-ounce cans diced tomatoes

1 14-ounce bottle ketchup

1 5-ounce bottle Worcestershire sauce

1 tablespoon vinegar

½ teaspoon red pepper powder

1 tablespoon dry mustard

Salt and Tabasco sauce to taste

[*This recipe calls for leftover smoked chicken and pork butt. It's a modified version of Brunswick Stew, a classic country dish that often includes squirrel or rabbit.*]

Chop chicken and pork finely; mix with remaining ingredients. Preheat grill to medium-low. Simmer for 3 to 4 hours on grill or cooktop. If stew is too thick, add more broth; if consistency is too thin, thicken with potato flakes. ❁

GRILLED PORK PANZANELLA

4 boneless pork chops, ½-inch-thick

⅔ cup Italian salad dressing

3 tablespoons balsamic vinegar

4 slices Italian bread, cut ½-inch-thick

1 10-ounce package Italian lettuce mix

1 cup canned cannellini beans, drained
and rinsed

1 cup ripe tomato, chopped

Freshly ground pepper

¼ cup Parmesan cheese, finely grated

Fresh basil for garnish

Combine Italian dressing and balsamic vinegar. Place ⅓ cup dressing mixture in self-sealing bag along with pork chops. Seal bag, and refrigerate for at least 30 minutes or as long as overnight. Cover and reserve remaining dressing.

Preheat grill to medium. Remove chops from marinade (discarding marinade), and grill over direct heat for 5 minutes per side until browned. Remove from grill, and keep warm.

Grill bread slices 2 to 3 minutes per side until toasted. Remove bread from grill, and cut it into ½-inch cubes. Meanwhile, combine lettuce, beans, and tomato in a large bowl. Add bread pieces and reserved dressing mixture; toss to coat all ingredients. Distribute lettuce mixture on four plates. Slice pork chops, and fan one pork chop over each salad. Garnish with black pepper, Parmesan, and fresh basil. ❁

4

PORK

MOJO CUBAN SANDWICHES

MARINADE

1 6-ounce can frozen orange
  juice concentrate, thawed

Juice of 3 key limes or 2 regular
  limes, about 3 to 4 tablespoons

¼ cup olive oil

3 large garlic cloves, chopped

1 tablespoon fresh oregano, minced,
  or 1½ teaspoons dried oregano

1 teaspoon kosher or sea salt

Several dashes of hot sauce
  (optional)

1 to 1¼ pounds pork tenderloin

2 tablespoons prepared yellow
  mustard

6 Cuban or French rolls (buns)

Dill pickle slices, enough to
  cover each sandwich

12 thin slices ham

12 thin slices Swiss cheese

Whisk together first seven ingredients. Set aside ¼ cup plus 2 tablespoons of mojo. Place tenderloin in plastic bag, and pour rest of mojo over it. Set aside at room temperature for 30 minutes, or refrigerate for up to several hours, and let sit at room temperature for 30 minutes before grilling.

Preheat grill to high. Remove tenderloin from marinade. Grill meat over high heat for 5 minutes, rolling it on all sides. Reduce heat to medium and continue rolling meat occasionally to cook evenly.

Pork is done when internal temperature reaches 155°F and center is barely pink. Let meat rest, covered with foil, for 10 minutes; then slice thinly.

Mix reserved mojo with mustard. Spread mojo-mustard mixture on both sides of bun. Layer pickles across bottom; add two ham slices, layer of pork tenderloin, and two cheese slices. Top with remaining bun. Toast each sandwich at edge of grill. Press until lightly brown and cheese melts slightly. Serve immediately. ❁

PISTACHIO SAUSAGE

3 pounds pork butt, coarsely ground
½ cup pistachios, shelled
1 clove of garlic, minced
1 tablespoon salt
1 tablespoon fresh parsley, chopped
1 teaspoon coarsely ground black pepper
½ teaspoon crushed red pepper
Additional black pepper to taste

[*Janeyce Michel-Cupito of the Powderpuff Barbeque Team submitted this recipe.*]

Combine pork, pistachios, garlic, salt, parsley, black pepper, and red pepper in bowl; mix well. Divide into four portions. Shape each portion into a roll 1½ inches in diameter; wrap in plastic wrap. Store in refrigerator until just before cooking. Discard plastic wrap. Coat surface of sausage with black pepper to taste. Grill over high heat until cooked through and browned, turning frequently. ❇

4

PORK

WISCONSIN-STYLE BRATS 'N KRAUT

12 ounces beer

½ large onion, chopped

3 tablespoons brown mustard

½ teaspoon caraway seeds

½ teaspoon ground coriander

12 fresh bratwursts, (4 to 5 ounces each), halved lengthwise

Prepare marinade by bringing first five ingredients to a boil in a saucepan; simmer mixture for 5 minutes. Add bratwursts to liquid; reduce heat to low; cover; and cook for 15 minutes. Remove pan from heat, leaving brats in liquid to steep.

Preheat grill to high. Prepare kraut relish by melting butter in a saucepan over medium heat. Stir in onion and caraway; cook 1 to 2 minutes until onion turns translucent. Add remaining relish ingredients, and heat through. Keep relish warm. Drain sausage, discarding marinade. Split halved brats in half again, lengthwise, resulting in four sausage spears. Grill brat pieces, uncovered, over high heat for about 2 minutes per side until well-browned. Toast rolls on edge of grill. To assemble sandwiches, spread both sides of each roll with mustard. To bottom of roll, add slice of cheese and build upward, topping each with eight brat pieces and a generous dollop of relish. Sprinkle chopped dill pickle over all; top with other half of roll. Repeat with remaining sandwiches, and serve. ✹

KRAUT RELISH

2 tablespoons butter

1 small onion, chopped

2 teaspoons caraway seeds

2 teaspoons brown mustard

2 cups sauerkraut, drained

Fresh ground black pepper

6 Kaiser or other large rolls

Additional brown mustard

6 thin slices Swiss or Provolone cheese

Dill pickle, chopped

"GREEN BAY" TAILGATING KIELBASA

10 horseshoe-shaped kielbasa
½ pound deli-style white American cheese, sliced
10 crusty French or Italian rolls
Favorite BBQ sauce

[*Courtesy of grilling fan Vincent and his fellow tailgaters from Hofstra University in New York.*]

Preheat grill to medium-high. Split each sausage lengthwise, taking care not to slice all the way through. Place kielbasas on grill, split sides down. After a few minutes, turn sausages over; place cheese on cut sides, and fold kielbasas closed; baste with BBQ sauce. Cook, turning occasionally, until sausages brown and cheese melts. Split open French rolls; toast rolls on edge of grill, if desired. Slather each roll with sauce, and place one sausage in each roll. Serve immediately. ✱

BACON-WRAPPED PORK & APPLE PATTIES

¾ cup quick-cooking rolled oats

½ teaspoon ground sage

½ teaspoon salt

¼ teaspoon pepper

¼ teaspoon dried thyme, crushed

⅓ cup applesauce

1 egg, slightly beaten

¼ cup scallion, minced

1 pound lean ground pork

4 slices bacon

1 large tart green apple, cored
and cut into thin wedges

½ medium onion, cut in small
wedges

1 tablespoon olive oil

Preheat grill to medium. In large bowl, combine oats, sage, salt, pepper, and thyme. Stir in applesauce, egg, and scallion; mix well. Stir in ground pork until well blended. Be sure not to overmix ground meat. Form into four patties about ¾ to 1 inch thick. Wrap bacon strip around each patty; secure with toothpick. Grill 4 to 5 minutes on each side.

Meanwhile in small skillet, cook and stir apples and onions in hot oil until tender. Sprinkle lightly with salt. Serve with pork and apple patties. ❀

4

PORK

Applesauce helps keep these burgers moist and flavorful. Remind diners to be careful of the toothpicks!

CB'S GRILLED VEGETABLE & SAUSAGE SOUP

[*Grilled veggies and sausage make this hearty soup a perfect meal for a cool fall day.* —CB]

2 tablespoons unsalted butter

1 teaspoon canola oil

1 medium yellow onion, chopped into bite-size chunks

1 large shallot, finely-chopped

4 inner stalks of celery, including leaves, roughly chopped into bite-size chunks

½ cup carrot slices or baby carrots

1 clove garlic, minced

Kosher salt to taste

Fresh ground black pepper to taste

2 tablespoons all-purpose flour

16 ounces chicken stock, unsalted

16 ounces vegetable stock, unsalted

1 cup baby zucchini squash

1 cup baby yellow squash

3 tablespoons extra virgin olive oil

1 medium-spicy sausage or bratwurst, precooked

1 cup of stale crusty bread, preferably ends

Preheat grill to high. On side burner, place large 8-quart stock pot on high heat. Add butter and canola oil to heated pot. Add onions and shallots, and stir, watching heat to ensure they caramelize but don't burn. Add celery after onions have begun to brown; let entire mixture sweat out excess moisture as celery cooks. Add carrots, and allow to cook until tender in remaining juices. Add garlic and salt and pepper to taste. Stir in flour, coating all vegetables; cook for 1 minute until vegetables begin to brown. Add both stocks to pot. (Make sure these are room temperature, as cold ingredients slow down the cooking!)

Place zucchini and squash in a large bowl; lightly toss with olive oil, salt, and pepper. Reduce grill heat to medium-high, and place vegetables on grill, turning as sear marks appear on veggies. (Note: you may wish to use a special stainless-steel grill plate that prevents veggies from dropping through grate, or place vegetables in a grill basket.) On the other side of grill, place precooked bratwurst or sausage, and brown until warm; remove to cutting board. Slice sausage into bite-size pieces, and add to soup, followed by grilled veggies. To serve, place a few chunks of bread in each bowl. (Note: you may wish to toast these on the grill first.) Ladle a generous portion of soup into each bowl, and serve. ❈

GRILLED HAM WITH LEMON-ORANGE GLAZE

7 pound bone-in smoked ham
2 tablespoons brown sugar
1 tablespoon ground coriander
1 tablespoon paprika
1 teaspoon cumin
½ teaspoon cinnamon
¼ teaspoon cloves

Preheat grill to medium (375°F to 425°F), and prepare for indirect cooking. Place drip pan in center, not over heat source. (For a gas grill, turn off the center burner; for a charcoal grill, bank coals on either side.) Score top and sides of ham with knife in a crisscross pattern. Mix remaining dry ingredients, and rub into surface of ham. Place ham, scored side up, in center of grill over drip pan. Cover, and grill for 1 to 1½ hours (add six to eight briquettes to charcoal grill if necessary to maintain heat), until internal temperature of ham is 140°F. While ham is grilling, prepare lemon-orange glaze. (See page 139.) Brush glaze over ham, and grill for 5 more minutes. Remove ham from grill, and let rest 15 minutes. ✳

LEMON-ORANGE GLAZE

¼ cup lemon marmalade

2 tablespoons orange juice

Combine marmalade and orange juice in a small bowl; brush over ham during last 5 minutes of grilling.

HAWAIIAN HAM

Juice reserved from 1 8¼-ounce can sliced pineapple
1 to 2 tablespoons soy sauce
1 teaspoon ground ginger
1 clove garlic, minced
Fully cooked ham, sliced into 4 steaks (1 inch thick)
Canned pineapple slices

Blend together pineapple juice, soy sauce, ginger, and garlic. Score ham in diamond pattern. Put steaks into a plastic storage bag, and add liquid. Marinate at least 30 minutes. Remove ham, and reserve marinade. Preheat grill to high. Grill ham until heated through, brushing often with marinade. After about 3 minutes on one side, turn steaks, and put pineapple slices directly on grill or in grill basket. Place pineapple slices on top of ham slices before serving. ✽

BOURBON-GLAZED ROTISSERIE HAM

1 fresh ham, about 10 pounds
1 cup bourbon
1 cup brown sugar
½ teaspoon ground cloves
Zest of 1 orange
⅓ cup steak sauce

Skin ham and score in a diamond pattern. Mix remaining ingredients in a bowl. Tie ham every 2 inches with string. Thread ham on a rotisserie spit rod, and fasten forks. If desired, insert a meat thermometer in center of thickest part of ham, making sure not to touch a bone. Place drip pan in grill. Grill ham for 4 to 5 hours until meat reaches an internal temperature of 170°F. During the last hour of grilling, brush glaze over all sides of ham. Continue to brush with glaze every 10 minutes. Remove from spit rod, and cut into thin slices. ❀

4

PORK

5 Poultry

(Left) BBQ Turkey Drumsticks, page 166

BBQ ORANGE CHICKEN

2½ pounds chicken parts

BBQ SAUCE
¼ cup vegetable oil
¼ cup frozen orange juice concentrate
½ cup white wine vinegar
¼ cup tomato paste
Zest from 1 orange

Preheat grill to high. In a medium bowl, mix together all sauce ingredients until smooth. Reduce heat to medium on one side; turn off heat on the other side. Place chicken pieces on grill away from heat, skin side down; cook 15 minutes. Turn chicken, and grill for 10 additional minutes. Brush chicken pieces with sauce, and turn occasionally, cooking for additional 10 minutes. ✳

GRILLED CHICKEN IN OLIVE OIL-CHIVES VINAIGRETTE

4 bone-in chicken breast quarters

Dip each piece of chicken in sauce (see recipe, below), and coat well. Marinate in refrigerator at least 4 hours or overnight.

Preheat grill to medium. Place chicken on grill, skin side up. Sprinkle with remaining ¾ teaspoon salt and ¼ teaspoon pepper. Grill, turning and basting with sauce every 10 minutes for about 1 hour or until internal temperature reaches approximately 150°F. ❋

OLIVE OIL-CHIVES VINAIGRETTE

6 tablespoons olive oil, divided
4 tablespoons red wine vinegar, divided
1 teaspoon salt, divided
½ teaspoon pepper, divided
¼ teaspoon dry mustard
1 clove garlic
Peel of 1 lemon
1 tablespoon chives, chopped

In food processor or blender, place 1 tablespoon of oil, 1 tablespoon of vinegar, and ¼ teaspoon each of salt, pepper, and mustard. Process 15 seconds. While processor is running, add 2 teaspoons olive oil; process 10 seconds. Add remaining 3 tablespoons vinegar, remaining 3 tablespoons oil, garlic, lemon peel, and chopped chives. Process 15 seconds more.

ISLAND GRILLED JERK CHICKEN

2 pounds boneless, skinless chicken breasts
⅓ cup soy sauce
2 tablespoons sesame oil
3 cloves garlic, chopped
3 scallions, chopped
3 tablespoons fresh thyme leaves
1½ teaspoons ground allspice
1½ teaspoons freshly ground pepper
½ teaspoon ground cinnamon
½ teaspoon ground red pepper
16 wooden skewers, soaked in water

Preheat the grill to medium-high. Wash the chicken, and pat it dry. Cut each chicken breast in half lengthwise, then into four strips; place the strips in a plastic storage bag. Combine the soy sauce and next eight ingredients in a blender; blend until smooth. Pour the mixture over the chicken, and tightly seal the bag. Turn the bag gently to coat the chicken. Marinate in the refrigerator for at least 1 hour and up to 24 hours. Thread chicken strips on skewers. Grill on each side until cooked.
Serve with Mango Papaya Relish. ❋

MANGO PAPAYA RELISH

(1½ cups)
1 ripe mango, peeled and diced
1 ripe papaya, peeled and diced
2 scallions, minced
¼ cup fresh cilantro, minced
2 teaspoons brown sugar
1 tablespoon lemon juice
Hot sauce to taste

Combine all ingredients in medium bowl; cover; and refrigerate at least 1 hour before serving.

CATALAN GRILLED CHICKEN LEGS

¼ teaspoon cayenne pepper

½ teaspoon cumin

½ teaspoon cinnamon

1 teaspoon salt

¼ teaspoon black pepper

4 chicken leg quarters

2 tablespoons olive oil

1 onion, medium sized, chopped

4 cloves garlic, chopped

¾ cup chorizo or other spicy
   sausage, chopped

1 28-ounce can whole, peeled
   tomatoes, drained and chopped

½ cup full-bodied red wine

½ cup pitted black olives, chopped

6 tablespoons pine nuts, toasted

5

POULTRY

Preheat the grill to high. In a small bowl, stir together the cayenne pepper, cumin, cinnamon, salt, and black pepper. Rub thoroughly over chicken leg quarters. Reduce grill to medium. Place chicken on grill, and cook, turning, until browned on all sides, about 10 minutes. While the chicken is grilling, warm the olive oil in a large pot over medium heat. Add the onions and garlic, and sauté until they begin to brown, about 4 minutes. Stir in the sausage, and continue to sauté for 3 minutes more. Stir in the tomatoes and wine, and bring the mixture to a simmer. When chicken is finished grilling, add it to the pot. Stir in the olives. Cover; reduce heat to medium-low; and simmer for 20 minutes.

To serve, put one piece of chicken in each of four shallow bowls. Top with the sauce, and sprinkle with toasted pine nuts. ❅

CHICKEN WITH GOAT CHEESE & ROASTED RED PEPPERS

4 boneless, skinless chicken breasts

¼ cup plus 2 tablespoons olive oil

2 red bell peppers, roasted

3 ounces fresh, soft goat cheese, sliced into rounds

1 teaspoon onion, chopped

1 teaspoon garlic, chopped

½ cup white wine

2 teaspoons fresh rosemary, chopped

½ stick butter, unsalted

Salt and pepper to taste

Sliced almonds, toasted

Preheat the grill to medium-high. Wash the chicken, and pat it dry. Brush chicken with 2 tablespoons of olive oil. Grill for 10 minutes or until no longer pink. Remove chicken to a baking dish, and top with the roasted pepper strips and cheese rounds. Bake at 350°F for 5 minutes or just until the cheese is heated through.

Sauté the onion and garlic in ¼ cup olive oil in a heavy skillet over high heat. Add the wine and rosemary. Cook for approximately 3 minutes. Gradually whisk in the butter. Season the mixture with salt and pepper; spoon over the chicken. Top with toasted almonds. ✳

CB'S MOROCCAN-SPICE GRILLED CHICKEN & PEACHES

1 15-ounce jar of peaches in
   natural juice (about 1 cup)
3 tablespoons curry powder
Kosher or sea salt to taste
Cooking oil spray
2 large boneless chicken breasts
2 tablespoons olive oil

1 clove garlic, finely chopped
1 tablespoon brown sugar
2 tablespoons balsamic vinegar
3 tablespoons mint or parsley, chopped

Pour peaches into a strainer with a bowl set underneath; remove the peaches to a plate, and reserve the juice. Rinse the chicken, and pat it dry; season with salt and curry powder. Let chicken reach room temperature, about 15 minutes.

Preheat one side of grill to high; reduce to medium-high when grilling. Preheat the other side to medium-low. Spray cooking oil on the chicken breasts, and place them on the hot side of grill. Grill for about 4 minutes per side, lifting chicken with tongs to check for burning. When both sides have dark grill marks, remove the chicken from the hot side of the grill, and place on the other side to "roast" until done, about 8 to 10 minutes.

In the meantime, warm the oil in a medium pan over medium-low heat. Add the garlic, and sauté until it begins to brown, about 1 to 2 minutes. Add the sugar, vinegar, and peach juice; reduce sauce while chicken cooks.

Using tongs, place the peach slices on hot side of grill to form grill marks. Turn the peaches just once to ensure uniform grill marks. When chicken is cooked to an internal temperature of approximately 150°F, remove and place on a warm plate until the internal temperature reaches approximately 160° to 170°. Cut chicken into pieces; place the grilled peaches on top; and pour the sauce over both. Garnish with mint or parsley. ❊

HERB & CHEESE-FILLED CHICKEN THIGHS

26 boneless, skinless chicken thighs
Herb and cheese filling (see recipe, opposite)

Stuff each thigh with approximately 2 tablespoons of the filling; then tie a string around each stuffed thigh to hold it together. (The chicken can be made 1 day ahead, covered with foil, and refrigerated.)

Preheat one side of grill to high. Grill the chicken, using indirect heat, to an internal temperature of 170°F. (Chicken can also be baked at 450° for about 35 minutes.)

Remove the chicken to a clean tray; and cover the tray with aluminum foil to retain heat. You can also place towels on top of the aluminum foil to help hold heat. During this time, the chicken will continue to rise in temperature another 5° to 10°. Serve chicken topped with your favorite tomato sauce or gravy. ❀

HERB & CHEESE FILLING

5 eggs, gently beaten

2¼ cups Italian-flavor bread crumbs

2¼ cups Parmesan cheese, shredded

1¼ cups provolone cheese, shredded

1¼ cups basil, chopped

1¼ cups parsley, chopped

2 ¼ tablespoons rosemary, finely chopped

Combine the filling ingredients in a mixing bowl, and follow instructions on opposite page for stuffing chicken thighs.

[*Marian, a long-time "Sizzle on the Grill" reader, sent me this do-ahead grill recipe that's perfect for a potluck supper or large holiday gathering.* —CB]

CB'S SOUVLAKI-STYLE GRILLED CHICKEN SKEWERS

2 ounces fresh lemon juice

4 ounces extra-virgin olive oil

1 tablespoon garlic, crushed

1 tablespoon cilantro, finely chopped

1 teaspoon Chinese dry mustard

1 teaspoon red pepper flakes

1 teaspoon fresh ginger (optional)

1 teaspoon kosher salt

1 teaspoon fresh ground black pepper

2 boneless, skinless chicken breasts

Preheat the grill to medium-high. Mix all ingredients except the chicken in a small mixing bowl, whisking to combine. Cut the chicken into 1-inch cubes. Place chicken into the bowl with the other ingredients; cover; and allow to marinate for at least 2 hours. While chicken is marinating, soak bamboo or wooden skewers in water.

Thread the chicken cubes onto the skewers; discard the marinade. Grill the chicken skewers over medium heat for 6 minutes on each side until the chicken has grill marks. Move skewers to indirect heat; cover grill; and continue cooking for 10 to 12 minutes or until done. Serve the skewers on top of rice, couscous, or cold pasta salad. ❀

CURRIED CHICKEN & SPINACH SALAD

4 bone-in chicken breasts

CURRY-MANGO CHUTNEY VINAIGRETTE

⅓ cup peanut oil

¼ cup rice vinegar

⅓ tablespoon prepared mango chutney

1 teaspoon curry powder

½ teaspoon salt

¼ teaspoon freshly ground black pepper

SALAD

12 ounces fresh spinach, washed and dried

3 grapefruits, peeled, white pith removed and sectioned

4 scallions, sliced

½ cup roasted peanuts, chopped

Put the chicken breasts into a glass dish. In a 2-cup measuring cup or a medium bowl, whisk together all of the ingredients for the vinaigrette. Pour half of the vinaigrette over the chicken, turning to coat all sides. Cover, and refrigerate for at least 1 hour or up to 24 hours. Cover the remaining vinaigrette, and refrigerate until needed.

Preheat the grill. Grill the chicken breasts for about 15 minutes or until the internal temperature registers 170°F in the center of the breast. Transfer the chicken to a cutting board. Remove the skin and, carefully pulling the chicken off the bone, slice each into a fan shape.

Whisk reserved vinaigrette to recombine. In a large bowl, toss the spinach, grapefruit sections, and scallions with the vinaigrette. Arrange the salad on a large serving platter. Place the chicken fans on top of the spinach. Sprinkle with peanuts, and serve. ✻

6 Servings • Prep: 15 min. • Marinate: 4 hr.–overnight • Grill: 25–30 min.

BBQ THAI CHICKEN SALAD

1 broiler-fryer chicken, about 3½ pounds

1 tablespoon curry powder

1 14-ounce can unsweetened coconut milk, regular or low fat

1 tablespoon lime juice

1 tablespoon fish sauce

3 garlic cloves, minced

¼ cup cilantro leaves, chopped

2 tablespoons brown sugar

12 red lettuce leaves, rinsed

1 medium head lettuce, shredded

1 large red bell pepper, sliced

½ cup mint leaves, torn

⅓ cup peanuts, finely chopped

SWEET & SOUR CILANTRO DRESSING

(1 cup)

⅔ cup rice vinegar

¼ cup sugar

¼ cup cilantro, minced

¼ teaspoons salt

½ teaspoons chili paste

⅓ cup safflower or canola oil

Rinse the chicken, and pat it dry. Split the chicken in half with a large, sharp knife. In a large bowl, whisk the curry powder into the coconut milk. Blend in the lime juice, fish sauce, garlic, cilantro, and brown sugar. Add the chicken, turning to coat it in the marinade. Cover, and refrigerate 4 hours to overnight.

Preheat the grill to medium. Place the chicken on the grill, skin side down. Turn after about 10 minutes, and continue cooking until the juices run clear or a fork can be inserted into the chicken with ease, about 30 minutes. Cool the chicken slightly; cut it into strips.

Prepare the dressing. Combine all of the ingredients; stir until the sugar dissolves. Arrange the red lettuce leaves on six plates. Combine the shreds of lettuce, bell pepper, and mint; distribute onto lettuce leaves. Scatter the chicken on top. Sprinkle the salad with peanuts; serve with dressing. ✾

MASTUR-K'S CHICKEN ON A STICK

1 medium to large boneless,
  skinless chicken breast
Garlic-pepper mix (Recipe follows.)
2 wooden skewers, soaked for at
  least 30 minutes

[*Mastur-K, also known as Kevin W,
is a "Sizzle on the Grill" reader
and contributor.* —CB]

Preheat grill to medium-low. Trim any fat from the chicken. Cut the fillet down the middle into two long strips. (Each piece should look like a chicken tender.) Place tenders in a clean kitchen towel, and pat them dry. Run skewers through both pieces, starting with smaller end. Place the skewers on a placemat or over the sink, and shake on as much garlic-pepper mix as desired. Grill skewers for 10 minutes on each side or until chicken is no longer pink in center. (Note: the small end of the chicken should be farther away from the center of the grill so that the larger end can cook evenly.) Serve with rice and vegetables. ✳

GARLIC-PEPPER MIX

2 tablespoons black peppercorns
1 tablespoon powdered garlic
1 tablespoon paprika
1 tablespoon Mrs. Dash spice
  mix (original flavor)

Put all ingredients into a spice or coffee grinder, and process until fine. Put the mixture in a shaker, and use it as you please.
Note: this recipe does not contain salt. You may add a tablespoon or two if desired.

2 Servings • Prep: 25 min. • Marinate: 1 hr.–overnight • Grill: 8–10 min. combined

GRILLED CHICKEN SKEWERS WITH GRILLED CAESAR SALAD

2 4-ounce boneless, skinless chicken breasts

1 cup BBQ sauce of your choice

2 whole heads romaine lettuce

½ cup extra-virgin olive oil

½ cup shallot, minced

½ cup fresh garlic, minced

Salt and pepper

Bamboo skewers soaked in white wine for 1 hour

1 prepared log herbed polenta

1 cup balsamic vinegar

1 jar of your favorite Caesar dressing

[*Provided by Erik Lind, 2006 Char-Broil Grilling Team Chef.*]

Cut the chicken breasts lengthwise into four equal slices. Place chicken in a plastic bag with the BBQ sauce; seal; and marinate for 1 to 2 hours or overnight. Cut the romaine heads in half lengthwise. Drizzle the olive oil over both sides. Spread the shallot, garlic, salt, and pepper over the cut side of the heads. Set lettuce aside.

Preheat grill to high. Place chicken on skewers, and grill until the meat reaches 165°F. Slice the polenta into ¼-inch slices, and spray with nonstick cooking spray. Grill polenta 5 to 8 minutes on each side to ensure even grill marks. To make the balsamic reduction, place vinegar in a pan over medium heat, and cook until it reduces into syrup. Cool, and reserve. Grill the romaine heads on both sides for 2 to 3 minutes until just wilted. Remove and slice lengthwise; then roughly chop. Toss lettuce very lightly with Caesar dressing. Place a small amount on each plate. Cut the polenta circles in half, and arrange them across the salad. Place the chicken skewers in an "X" over the salad, and drizzle with the balsamic reduction. ✳

24 Servings • Prep: 25 min. • Marinate: 2 hr. • Grill: 1 hr.

159

DO-AHEAD MINCED BBQ CHICKEN

1 quart apple cider vinegar

⅓ cup low-sodium chicken broth

⅓ teaspoon onion salt

1 teaspoon coarsely ground fresh pepper

2 bay leaves

12 chicken leg quarters

24 sandwich buns

1 cup Dijon mustard

In a large saucepan, mix together the vinegar, chicken broth, onion salt, pepper, and bay leaves. Bring to a boil over high heat. Place the chicken in a bowl, and pour the hot vinegar mixture over it. Cover, and marinate in the refrigerator for at least 2 hours.

Preheat the grill to medium. Place the chicken on the grill, skin side up. Pour 2 cups of the marinade in a small saucepan, and bring to a boil on the grill. Grill the chicken, turning and basting with the boiled marinade every 10 to 15 minutes for about 1 hour or until the internal temperature reaches 165°F.

Remove the chicken from the grill, and let it cool for about 10 minutes. Cut the chicken from the bone; discarding the bones and skin. Place the meat, four quarters at a time, into a food processor and pulse 3 or 4 times until the chicken is coarsely chopped. (Chop with a knife if a processor is not available.) Repeat this with the remaining chicken. (There should be about 9 cups.)

Boil the remaining marinade to reduce it to 1¼ cups; pour over the minced chicken. Serve on buns spread with mustard. Garnish with a dill pickle slice, if desired. ✳

BEER-CAN CHICKEN

1 whole chicken (4 to 5 pounds)
2 teaspoons vegetable oil
1 16-ounce can beer

In a small bowl, combine the rub ingredients. (See opposite page.) Wash the chicken, and pat it dry. Rub the entire chicken with vegetable oil and season it with the rub, inside and out.

Preheat the grill to medium. Pour half of the beer out of the can, and carefully place the half-full can inside the cavity of the chicken. Note: the can will be almost completely covered by the chicken. Transfer the bird to the grill, keeping the can upright. Grill for 1½ to 2 hours or until the internal temperature reaches 180°F in the thickest part of the thigh and the meat is no longer pink. Carefully remove the chicken with the can from the grill using protective mitts. Liquid remaining in the can will be hot; be careful not to spill it. Let the chicken rest for about 10 minutes before lifting it from the can. Discard the beer. Cut the chicken into serving pieces. ❋

RUB 1

1 teaspoon dry mustard

¼ cup onion, minced

1 teaspoon paprika

1 teaspoon kosher salt

4 small cloves garlic, minced

½ teaspoon ground coriander

½ teaspoon ground cumin

½ teaspoon freshly ground
  black pepper

RUB 2

3 tablespoons paprika

2 tablespoons sugar

1 tablespoon salt

2 teaspoons coarsely ground
  black pepper

1 teaspoon onion powder

1 teaspoon garlic powder

1 teaspoon ground red
  pepper (cayenne)

[*Use either of these rubs for this moist and flavorful chicken, or try your own favorite dry seasoning.* —CB]

CB'S GRILLED DUCK BREASTS WITH SWEET-POTATO FRIES

1 teaspoon garlic powder

1 teaspoon dried cumin

1 teaspoon Chinese-style dry
mustard

1 teaspoon dry ginger

1 teaspoon curry powder

1 teaspoon kosher salt or
sea salt

1 teaspoon fresh ground black
pepper

2 medium-size duck breasts,
approximately 6–8 ounces each

1 tablespoons high-heat
cooking oil (preferably canola
or grapeseed)

1 medium-size sweet potato

4 tablespoons Parmesan cheese

2 tablespoons flat leaf parsley,
chopped

4 tablespoons extra virgin
olive oil

Combine the first seven ingredients in a bowl. Rinse duck, and pat it dry. Gently rub the spice mixture onto the duck. You may also want to pierce the skin in several places to help the fat escape. Let duck rest at room temperature for about 20 minutes. Cut the sweet potato into equal-size slices, and place in cold, salted water.

Preheat the grill to high. Preheat a cast-iron skillet to hot; add 1 teaspoon of canola oil. Gently place duck in the skillet, fat side down. Cook, without turning, for about 3 to 4 minutes. When skin is golden, turn the breasts over, and sear the meat for an additional minute; then lift and place meat side down on the grill. Reserve the duck fat in the skillet. Reduce grill heat to medium-low, and close the lid. Cook duck for 4 minutes; then remove, and cover until meat reaches 135°F for rare.

Add the remaining canola oil to duck fat in skillet, and allow to heat to smoking point. Remove potato slices from the water; pat very dry; then place about half of the slices in the skillet. Cook fries in batches until tender, but not browned. When all the fries are done, return them to the hot oil to brown; drain on paper towels. Sprinkle fries with Parmesan and parsley, and arrange them on a plate. Slice the duck meat, and arrange on plate with the fries. Drizzle with olive oil, and serve.❋

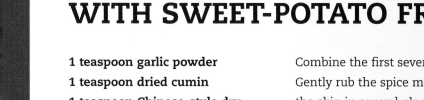

FIRST-PRIZE GRILLED TURKEY BREAST

1 bone-in turkey breast (3½ to 4 pounds)

This recipe by Tye Rinner won first prize in the Autumn 2000 Iowa Farm Bureau Cookout Contest.

MARINADE

¾ cup orange juice

¾ cup soy sauce

¼ cup honey

½ cup scallions, chopped

4 cloves garlic, crushed

2 teaspoons freshly ground black pepper

2 teaspoons ground ginger

MANGO-PAPAYA RELISH

(1½ cups)

1 mango, peeled and diced

1 papaya, peeled and diced

2 scallions, minced

¼ cup cilantro, minced

2 teaspoons brown sugar

1 tablespoon lemon juice

Hot sauce to taste

Combine all ingredients; cover; and refrigerate the mixture for at least 1 hour before serving.

Mix the orange juice, soy sauce, honey, scallions, garlic, and seasonings together. Reserve ¼ cup of marinade. Place the remaining marinade in a large plastic bag. Add the turkey breast; seal; and marinate in refrigerator for 12 to 24 hours, turning the sealed bag every few hours. Remove the turkey from the marinade, and drain. Prepare the grill for indirect-heat cooking. Place the turkey, breast side up, on grill over a drip pan. Cover, and grill the turkey breast for 1¼ to 1¾ hours. During last 30 minutes, brush the turkey breast with the reserved ¼ cup of marinade. Cook until a meat thermometer inserted in the thickest portion of the breast registers 170°F. Remove the turkey breast from the grill, and let stand for 15 minutes before carving. Serve with mango-papaya relish ❋

5

POULTRY

PINEAPPLE-MUSTARD TURKEY BREAST

⅓ cup pineapple preserves
1 teaspoon fresh lemon juice
2 teaspoon Dijon-style mustard
1 bone-in turkey breast (3–4 pounds)

Prepare the grill for indirect-heat cooking. In a small bowl, combine the preserves, lemon juice, and mustard. Place the turkey, skin side up, on the rack over a drip pan. Cover, and grill the turkey breast 1 to 1¼ hours, brushing the pineapple glaze on the breast 30 minutes before the end of the grilling time. Cook until a meat thermometer inserted in the thickest portion of the breast registers 170°F. Remove the turkey breast from the grill, and let stand for 15 minutes. To serve, slice the breast, and arrange on a platter with sliced fresh fruit. ✳

CURRIED TURKEY TENDERLOINS

1 pound turkey tenderloins
¼ cup vegetable oil
⅓ tablespoon fresh lime juice
½ tablespoon onion, minced
½ teaspoon curry powder
½ teaspoon grated lime zest
½ teaspoon garlic powder
¼ teaspoon salt
¼ teaspoon cumin
¼ teaspoon ground cinnamon
¼ teaspoon freshly ground
  black pepper

Butterfly the tenderloins by cutting each tenderloin lengthwise, taking care not to cut all the way through. Between two sheets of wax paper, gently flatten the butterflied tenderloins using the smooth side of a meat tenderizer.

In a self-closing plastic bag, combine all ingredients. Close the bag, and refrigerate for 1 to 2 hours.

Preheat the grill to medium. Grill the tenderloins 5 to 6 minutes per side or until the internal temperature reaches 170°F. ❋

BBQ TURKEY DRUMSTICKS

4 pounds turkey drumsticks

Arrange the turkey drumsticks in a foil-lined roasting pan. Pour the barbecue sauce (see opposite page) over the drumsticks; cover; and marinate them for 2 hours in the refrigerator. Turn the drumsticks occasionally in the sauce. Remove them from the refrigerator.

Preheat grill to low. Grill the drumsticks until browned, about 7 minutes on each side. Turn and baste them frequently. Continue to grill over low heat for about 1 hour or until the internal temperature registers 180°F. ❋

BBQ SAUCE

½ clove garlic, minced
1 cup chili sauce or ketchup
¼ cup vegetable oil
⅓ cup cider vinegar
¼ cup onion, chopped
1 tablespoon Worcestershire sauce
½ teaspoon salt
¼ teaspoon freshly ground pepper
½ teaspoon dried thyme

Combine all ingredients in a small saucepan. Simmer, uncovered, over low heat for 15 to 20 minutes.

GRILLED TURKEY & VEGETABLE SALAD

½ cup balsamic vinegar

¼ cup olive oil

1 teaspoon garlic, chopped

¾ teaspoon dried basil

½ teaspoon red pepper flakes, crushed

¼ teaspoon salt

1 pound turkey tenderloins, butterflied

2 small eggplants

2 medium zucchinis cut into ½-inch diagonal slices

1 red bell pepper, seeded

1 yellow bell pepper, seeded

8 small red onion wedges

Vegetable and cooking spray

In a small bowl, whisk together the vinegar, oil, garlic, basil, pepper flakes, and salt; set this aside to use for the marinade and dressing. In a large, self-closing plastic bag, place the tenderloins with ¼ cup of the dressing; seal the bag. Refrigerate for 1 hour, turning the bag several times.

Pierce the eggplants with a fork, and place them on a paper towel in a microwave oven. Cook on high for 1 to 2 minutes, or until soft. Allow them to cool. Make four lengthwise slices in each eggplant, leaving the stem end intact to fan out the slices.

In a large bowl, combine the eggplant, zucchini, red and yellow pepper, and onion with ¼ cup of the dressing. Cover and refrigerate the vegetables for 1 hour, stirring gently a few times. Cover and refrigerate the remaining dressing.

Remove the tenderloins from the bag; discard the remaining marinade. Place the tenderloins on the grill. Fan out the eggplants, and place them with the other vegetables around the turkey. Grill for 5 minutes; turn; and continue cooking for 4 to 5 minutes, or until the turkey is no longer pink in center. Watch the vegetables closely to prevent burning.

To serve, slice the tenderloins and peppers into ½-inch slices. Arrange the tenderloins on four plates; surround them with grilled vegetables; and drizzle them with 1 teaspoon dressing each. ❋

SPICY LIME & CILANTRO TURKEY FAJITAS

1 tablespoon paprika

½ teaspoon onion salt

½ teaspoon garlic powder

½ teaspoon cayenne pepper

½ teaspoon fennel seeds, crushed

½ teaspoon dried thyme

¼ teaspoon white pepper

1 pound turkey tenderloins, butterflied

Juice of 1 lime

1 cup sour cream (regular or reduced fat)

¼ cup scallions, thinly sliced

¼ cup fresh cilantro, finely chopped

1 4-ounce can green chilies, drained

1 plum tomato, seeded, finely chopped

½ teaspoon black pepper

¼ teaspoon cayenne pepper

4 pitas, round, cut in half

½ cup lettuce, shredded

In a shallow dish, combine the paprika, onion salt, garlic powder, cayenne pepper, fennel, thyme, and white pepper. Rub the mixture over the turkey; cover; and refrigerate for 1 hour.

Preheat grill to medium-high. Grill the turkey, turning once, for 5 to 6 minutes or until a meat thermometer registers 170°F in the thickest part of the tenderloin. Remove turkey to a serving plate, and squeeze lime juice over them. Slice the tenderloins on the diagonal into ¼-inch slices.

Meanwhile, in a small bowl, combine the sour cream, onions, cilantro, chilies, tomato, and black and cayenne peppers. To serve, fill each pita halfway with turkey, and top with the sour cream sauce. Add the shredded lettuce. ❋

4 Servings • Prep: 10 min. • Marinate: 1 hr.–overnight • Grill: 60 min.

171

ASIAN BBQ TURKEY THIGHS

¾ cup plain barbecue sauce

¼ cup scallions, sliced

3 tablespoons soy sauce

½ tablespoon sesame seeds, toasted

1 teaspoon garlic, minced

¼ teaspoon ground ginger

2 pounds turkey thighs, skin and fat removed

In a 2-cup measure, combine the barbecue sauce, onions, soy sauce, sesame seeds, garlic, and ginger. Remove ⅓ cup of the mixture; cover the rest; and refrigerate. Pierce holes in the turkey using tines of a fork. In a self-closing plastic bag, combine the thighs and the remaining marinade. Seal the bag and refrigerate 1 hour or overnight, turning occasionally to marinate the thighs.

Preheat grill to medium. Cook the thighs over medium heat for 25 to 30 minutes per side or until a meat thermometer inserted in the thickest portion of the thigh registers 180°F. During the last 10 minutes of cooking, brush the thighs with the reserved marinade. Serve hot with your favorite rice dish and vegetable, if desired. ❋

5

POULTRY

BBQ TURKEY BURGERS WITH CREAMY COLESLAW

2 pounds ground turkey
1 small onion, minced
½ cup fresh bread crumbs
1 small onion, sliced thin
6 6-inch pita loaves, split

COLESLAW
⅓ cup mayonnaise
½ tablespoon cider vinegar
1 teaspoon sugar
1 teaspoon Dijon mustard
3 cups cabbage, finely shredded
½ cup carrot, peeled coarsely grated

In a large bowl, whisk together the mayonnaise, vinegar, sugar, and mustard. Add the remaining coleslaw ingredients; salt and pepper to taste. Note: the coleslaw may be made 4 hours ahead and chilled.

BARBECUE SAUCE
2 cloves garlic, minced
½ teaspoon salt
¼ cup Worcestershire sauce
¼ cup ketchup
2 tablespoons light soy sauce
1 teaspoon chili powder
¼ teaspoon ground cumin
¼ teaspoon Tabasco sauce
Salt and pepper

In a small bowl, mash the minced garlic with salt to form a paste. Stir in the Worcestershire, ketchup, soy sauce, chili powder, cumin, Tabasco, salt, and pepper. Blend until smooth.

In a large bowl, stir the turkey, onion, breadcrumbs, and ¼ cup barbecue sauce until well combined. Form the mixture into six ¾-inch-thick patties. Divide the remaining sauce in half; cover; and reserve.

Preheat the grill to medium-high. Grill the turkey burgers, brushing them frequently with barbecue sauce, for about 6 minutes on each side or until internal temperature reaches 165°F. Drizzle the turkey burgers with the remaining sauce, and place them in the pita pockets. Serve with coleslaw. ❊

ALL-AMERICAN TURKEY BURGERS

1 pound ground turkey
½ cup onion, chopped
1 clove garlic, minced
¼ cup ketchup
⅛ teaspoon pepper
4 Kaiser rolls, sliced
4 leaves lettuce
4 slices red ripe tomato
4 thin slices onion

Preheat the grill. In a medium-size bowl, combine the turkey, onion, garlic, ketchup, and pepper. Evenly divide the turkey mixture into four burgers, approximately 3 inches in diameter. Grill the turkey burgers 5 to 6 minutes per side until they reach 165°F on a food thermometer and the turkey is no longer pink in the center. To serve, place each turkey burger on the bottom half of a Kaiser roll, and top it with lettuce, tomato, and onion and the remaining half of the roll. ❇

BURRITO TURKEY BURGERS

Vegetable cooking spray

2 pounds ground turkey

4 ounces green chilies, chopped and drained

1 cup onion, chopped

1 ounce taco seasoning mix

8 8-inch flour tortillas

16 ounces refried beans

Lettuce, shredded

½ cup cheddar cheese, grated and divided

2 cups salsa

Preheat the grill to medium-high. In a medium bowl, combine the turkey, chilies, onion, and seasoning mix. Evenly divide the turkey into eight rectangular burgers. Grill the burgers for 3 to 4 minutes; turn them; and continue cooking for 2 to 3 minutes or until they reach 165°F on a meat thermometer and the turkey is no longer pink in the center.

Remove the burgers and keep them warm. Heat the tortillas according to the package directions. Spread each tortilla with ¼ cup refried beans, and sprinkle with lettuce. Place the burgers in the center of each tortilla, and sprinkle 1 tablespoon of cheese over the top. Fold the sides of the tortilla over the burger to create a burrito. Serve with salsa. ❈

CLASSIC SMOKED TURKEY

1 12-pound or larger turkey,
    defrosted
Peanut oil
Salt and pepper
Poultry seasoning, if desired
1 stick butter
Wood chips (pecan, hickory, or oak)

Rub the turkey with peanut oil; then season with salt, pepper, and the poultry seasoning or rub of your choice. Place the turkey in a heavy foil pan. Cut the butter in large chunks, and place them in the pan. Tent the turkey with a piece of foil placed loosely over top; don't seal it completely.

Prepare the fire with wood chips according to your smoker's directions. Place the pan with the turkey in the cooking chamber, and smoke the turkey at 200°F to 250°F, basting every 3 hours with the butter drippings from the bottom of the pan. Smoke the turkey for about 45 to 60 minutes per pound or until a meat thermometer inserted in the breast registers 165°F. ❊

JUDGE STEVE'S WORLD-FAMOUS RECIPE FOR SMOKING TURKEY

1 13–20 pound turkey, preferably natural (not self-basting), fully defrosted

BRINE
½ gallon apple juice
½ gallon orange juice
1 pound brown sugar
¾ cup kosher salt
6 to 8 cinnamon sticks, broken in pieces
15 to 20 whole cloves

In a 6-gallon food-grade plastic container or bucket lined with a clean plastic garbage bag, mix together the first four brine ingredients; then add the cinnamon and cloves. Remove the giblets and neck from both cavities; place the turkey in the container. Add 1 gallon of water, and mix again. Make sure the bird is fully immersed in the liquid, adding more juice or water if necessary. Brine the turkey for at least 6 hours or overnight in the refrigerator.

About 30 to 45 minutes before smoking, remove the turkey from the brine; rinse it well; pat dry; and let dry at room temperature.

Prepare enough charcoal to maintain a temperature of 350°F for 2 to 3 hours for a 13-pound turkey—or as much as 5 hours for a bird weighing 20 pounds or more. Add pecan, cherry, or other hardwood chunks on top of the coals.

Cook the turkey, breast side up, until the breast reaches a minimum of 165°F on an instant-read thermometer. Remove the turkey from the smoker, and let it rest for 30 minutes before carving. ❈

THE BIG EASY SOUTHERN-STYLE TURKEY

⅔ cup vinaigrette dressing

⅓ cup dry sherry

2 teaspoons lemon-pepper seasoning

1 teaspoon garlic powder

1 teaspoon onion powder

1 teaspoon cayenne pepper

10- to 12-pound natural turkey (not self-basting)

Remove the giblets and neck from both cavities; rinse the turkey well with cold water; and thoroughly pat it dry with paper towels. In a medium bowl, mix the vinaigrette, sherry, and seasonings together. Strain the marinade; and inject mixture into the turkey breast, thighs, and legs using a marinade injector. Place the bird in a large plastic bag; refrigerate; and let marinate for at least 2 hours. Turn the bag, massaging turkey occasionally.

Drain marinade from the turkey; discard the marinade. Place the turkey in the fryer basket of The Big Easy, breast side up; insert meat thermometer in breast. Cook the turkey for approximately 10 minutes per pound or until the thermometer registers 165°F. Carefully remove the turkey from the basket, and place on a platter. Allow the turkey to rest for 15 to 20 minutes before carving. ✳

5

POULTRY

Thanks to The Big Easy, Char-Broil's new infrared turkey fryer, you can prepare juicy, flavorful, crisp-skinned "fried" turkey in a fraction of the time— and without a drop of oil. The recipe times here and on the next two pages have all been adapted for cooking in The Big Easy. —CB

8–10 Servings • Prep: 15 min. • Marinate: 1 hr.–overnight • Cook: 2–2½ hr.

THE BIG EASY ASIAN-STYLE TURKEY

1 10- to 12-pound
natural turkey,
(not self-basting)
2 tablespoons salt
1 tablespoon freshly
ground black pepper
3 tablespoons wasabi
powder

BRINE

1 cup low-sodium soy
sauce
⅔ cup sugar
⅔ cup salt

Remove the giblets and neck from both cavities. Rinse the turkey with cold water. Cut off the wing tips and little tail, as they may be caught in The Big Easy's fryer basket. Combine the soy sauce, sugar, and salt in a 40- to 60-quart pot. Submerge the turkey in water. Add enough water to cover it. Stir the liquid to distribute the seasonings evenly. Cover, and refrigerate the turkey for 8 to 24 hours.

Remove the turkey from the brine; then rinse it well, removing all sugar and salt. Pat the interior and exterior dry with paper towels. Drain the brining liquid.

Stir together the salt, black pepper, and wasabi powder. Rub the spice mixture all over the turkey, inside and out. Place the turkey in fryer basket, breast side up; insert meat thermometer in breast. Cook the turkey for approximately 10 minutes per pound or until the internal temperature reaches a minimum of 165°F. Carefully remove turkey from the basket. Allow the turkey to cool for 15 to 20 minutes before carving. ✵

THE BIG EASY GINGER & ROSEMARY TURKEY

10- to 12-pound natural turkey (not self-basting)

¼ cup fresh ginger, peeled and sliced

2 tablespoons fresh rosemary, crushed

6 cloves fresh garlic, peeled

¼ cup fresh garlic, minced

2 tablespoons kosher salt

2 teaspoons freshly ground black pepper

Remove the giblets and neck; rinse the turkey well with cold water; and thoroughly pat it dry with paper towels. Take care to dry both inside and outside. Fill the cavity with the ginger, rosemary, and garlic cloves. Mix together the minced garlic, salt, and pepper, and rub this on the exterior of the bird. Do not truss or tie the legs together. Cut off the wing tips and the little tail as they may get caught in The Big Easy's fryer basket. Cover the pan, and place it in the refrigerator overnight.

Place the turkey in the basket, breast side up; insert a meat thermometer in the breast. Cook the turkey for approximately 10 minutes per pound or until the internal temperature is a minimum of 165°F. Carefully remove the turkey from the basket. Allow turkey to rest for 15 to 20 minutes before carving. ❈

5

POULTRY

6 Seafood

(Left) Grilled Swordfish with Citrus Salsa, page 200

PRAWNS WITH PARMESAN-HERB BASTE

12 wooden skewers

**¼ cup Parmesan
cheese, freshly grated**

2 tablespoons olive oil

2 tablespoons red wine vinegar

1½ teaspoons dried basil

**1 teaspoon coarsely ground
black pepper**

**24 Alaska Spot Prawns or
jumbo shrimp, peeled, tails on**

Soak skewers in water for at least 30 minutes. Blend grated cheese, olive oil, vinegar, basil, and pepper. Place two prawns on each skewer, carefully piercing through both head and tail sections. Transfer skewers to baking tray; brush each prawn with parmesan mixture; cover and refrigerate for 30 minutes. Reserve any remaining baste.

Preheat grill to medium-high. Place skewers directly over heat on well-oiled grill; cook for 3 to 4 minutes. Turn once; brush with remaining baste; and continue to cook for 3 to 4 minutes or until prawns turn pink and are opaque throughout. ✻

CHIPOTLE SHRIMP

2 teaspoons olive oil

1 cup onion, finely chopped

4 garlic cloves, minced

2 teaspoons ground cumin

1 teaspoon dried oregano

1 cup water

¼ cup apple cider vinegar

2 teaspoons canned chipotle chilies, chopped

1½ pounds uncooked jumbo shrimp, peeled and deveined

¼ cup orange juice

2 teaspoons light brown sugar

Heat oil in heavy skillet over medium heat. Add onion; sauté for about 10 minutes or until golden brown. Add garlic, cumin, and oregano; stir 1 minute. Transfer mixture to blender. Add water, vinegar, and chipotles to blender; puree until smooth. Transfer half of puree to medium bowl; cool. Add shrimp to bowl, and toss to coat. Cover; chill 2 hours.

Pour remaining puree into heavy medium saucepan. Add orange juice and brown sugar; bring to a boil. Reduce heat; simmer for about 10 minutes or until glaze is slightly thickened and reduced to ½ cup. Remove from heat, and cool.

Preheat grill to medium-high. Remove shrimp from marinade; pat dry using paper towels. Lightly brush shrimp with orange juice glaze. Grill shrimp, brushing once more with marinade, until shrimp are opaque in center, about 2 minutes per side. Transfer to platter. ❊

6

SEAFOOD

CB'S GRILLED SEA SCALLOPS WITH LEMON & FENNEL SAUCE

[*Scallops can be seared on cast-iron grates when using a charcoal or gas grill. If you have one of the new Char-Broil infrared grills, use a medium-high setting.* —CB]

1 large lemon with unblemished peel

2 egg yolks

2 teaspoons canola oil, or cooking oil spray

1 medium-large fennel bulb, sliced lengthwise and cut into bite-size strips

1 cup unsalted chicken broth

$\frac{1}{8}$ teaspoon cinnamon or nutmeg

10 large sea scallops, fresh or thawed

1½ cups dry white wine, champagne, or dry vermouth

½ tablespoon corn starch

2 teaspoons sea salt or kosher salt

2 teaspoons freshly ground black pepper

Using a citrus zester or grater, create "frizzles" from lemon rind. Juice remainder of lemon, and reserve.

In a small bowl, add egg yolks and about 1 tablespoon of lemon juice. Mix using a whisk—do not froth.

Preheat oven to medium-high. In a medium-size saucepan, add 1 tablespoon of canola oil. Add fennel, and heat slightly; then add wine and lemon zest. Bring mixture to a boil; cook until reduced by half and fennel is fork-tender.

Add chicken broth and nutmeg or cinnamon to saucepan, stir until well blended. Return to boil; then reduce heat to medium. Continue to cook until sauce is reduced by about half.

Using a large spoon, add some of the sauce reduction to the egg and lemon-juice mixture before adding it to the saucepan. (This will prevent yolks from scrambling.) Add mixture to saucepan, and continue to cook on medium heat. Sauce should be a creamy consistency. If sauce is not coming together, add a very small amount of cornstarch. Add lemon juice and sea salt to taste.

Preheat grill to medium-high. Lightly spray sea scallops with cooking oil on both sides; place on grill. Let scallops develop grill marks on one side, about 3 minutes.

Using a metal spatula coated with canola oil, gently, but swiftly, slide spatula under each scallop; then turn scallop using tongs. Once grill marks appear, turn scallop and place on "fresh" section of grates; cook for approximately 3 minutes.

When scallops are marked, remove from grill and place on warmed plate. Cover, and set aside. Ladle a generous portion of sauce on each plate, and place three to five scallops on plate with best grill marks showing. Note: if you cover scallops after grilling and hold them on a warm plate, they should be fully cooked. If not, simply place in sauce to finish cooking. Ladle small amount of sauce over scallops; garnish with fennel fronds or parsley. ❊

BOB & LEE'S ROSEMARY & GARLIC GRILLED SHRIMP

1 pound raw shrimp, peeled, tails on

1 clove garlic, minced or chopped

1 teaspoon dried rosemary, crushed, or 2 teaspoons fresh rosemary, finely chopped

1 teaspoon dried basil, or 2 teaspoons fresh basil, finely chopped

1 teaspoon freshly ground pepper

⅛ teaspoon kosher or sea salt

1 to 2 teaspoons extra-virgin olive oil

[*Marinating time can be overnight if preparing on a stove or 1 hour before grilling.*]

Mix first five ingredients together in a large bowl; marinate in refrigerator 1 hour or overnight. Preheat grill to medium heat. Just before grilling, add salt and 1 to 2 teaspoons of extra-virgin olive oil to shrimp mixture; mix to coat well.

Place shrimp on grill, and cook for 3 minutes on each side. Serve. ❋

THAI SHRIMP

15 to 20 shrimp, tails on
1 tablespoon Cajun spice mix
1 cup white wine
1 teaspoon fresh cilantro, chopped
1 teaspoon Tabasco sauce
½ teaspoon chili paste
½ teaspoon lime juice
1 pinch of chili flakes

6

SEAFOOD

Preheat grill to medium-high. Place shrimp in medium-size bowl. Sprinkle Cajun spice on shrimp, and toss until lightly coated. Add remaining six ingredients to medium saucepan.

Grill shrimp over medium-high heat, turning once, for 4 to 5 minutes or until pink. Place saucepan containing sauce ingredients over heat. Place shrimp in sauce; bring to a boil for about 2 minutes. Serve. ❋

MICK'S SEAFOOD MIX

¼ cup olive oil

1 cup onions, roughly chopped

5 or 6 large cloves garlic, thinly sliced

3 or 4 Andouille or other spicy, precooked sausages

1 20-ounce can diced tomatoes, drained

10 or 12 fresh basil leaves, shredded

Salt and ground pepper to taste

8 to 10 Little Neck clams

20 fresh mussels

1 pound (16–20) large shrimp

¼ cup white wine, champagne, or chicken broth

1 pound cooked linguini

1 beer for drinking while preparing. Okay, 2.

Preheat grill to medium. Heat olive oil in pan on stove or side burner of grill. Add onions and garlic to pan; cook until soft and they smell really good. (If you have kids, expect them to start asking "what's for dinner?" about now.)

Brown sausage on grill; remove; and cut into bite-size pieces. Put sausage, onions, and garlic in a medium bowl. Add tomatoes, basil, salt, and pepper; mix. Clean mussels and clams under cold running water. Peel shrimp.

Heat grill to medium. Make basket out of heavy-duty aluminum foil, and place mussels, clams, and shrimp in center. Pour sauce on top; add wine. Bring foil together to seal. Place foil packet directly on grill; cook for 10 minutes. Using tongs, carefully shake packet; grill for another 5 minutes. When clams and mussels are open and shrimp is pink, put on large platter. Serve with linguine and crusty bread. ✽

GARLIC-LIME ALASKA PRAWNS WITH AVOCADO CREAM

1½ tablespoons kosher salt

1½ tablespoons sugar

1½ pounds peeled Alaska Spot Prawns, or large shrimp, tails on

¼ cup olive oil

¼ cup fresh cilantro, chopped

3 cloves garlic, peeled and minced

2 teaspoons grated lime peel

½ teaspoon fresh-ground pepper

Avocado Cream (See recipe on page 292.)

In a bowl, combine salt and sugar. Rinse prawns; pat dry. Add prawns to salt-sugar mixture; stir gently to coat. Cover, and refrigerate for up to 1 hour.

Rinse prawns well, and then drain; rinse and dry bowl. Preheat grill to high. In another bowl, combine olive oil, cilantro, garlic, lime peel, and pepper. Add prawns, and mix to coat. Thread prawns on metal or soaked wooden skewers, running them through each prawn at the tail and head to form a C-shape.

Lay skewers on well-oiled grill grates. Close lid on gas grill. Cook, turning once, just until prawns are opaque throughout, about 3 to 5 minutes total. Push prawns off skewers, and arrange on platter. Set avocado cream alongside.

Note: a brief cure in salt and sugar adds flavor to prawns and makes them more tender. You can cure and marinate the prawns up to 1 day ahead. Chill in an airtight container. ✳

LOBSTER TAILS WITH BROWN SUGAR SAUCE

4 lobster tails
3 tablespoons brown sugar
¼ cup butter
¼ cup breadcrumbs

DIPPING SAUCE
¼ cup butter
2 cloves garlic, crushed
1 teaspoon parsley, chopped
Salt and pepper

Combine ingredients for lobster, brown sugar, butter, and crumbs in a small saucepan. Place pan over medium heat, stirring occasionally, until butter is melted and sugar is dissolved.

Preheat grill to medium. Cook lobster tails on grill for 4 to 6 minutes.

In a separate saucepan, combine ingredients for dipping sauce. Heat until butter is melted. Remove lobster from grill, and baste with lobster mixture. Serve with dipping sauce. ❋

SALMON TARRAGON

4 salmon fillets (6–8 ounces each)

Salt and pepper

1 medium onion, diced

2 teaspoons dried tarragon

2 tablespoons shallots, chopped

½ cup white wine

2 tablespoons Dijon mustard

¼ cup chicken stock

¼ cup light cream

Preheat grill to medium-high. Sprinkle salmon fillets with salt and pepper; let stand for 5 to 10 minutes.

Add remaining ingredients to medium saucepan; bring to a slow boil.

Grill salmon over medium-high heat until flesh is just opaque throughout. Drizzle with sauce, and serve. ❋

CB'S GRILLED WILD SALMON WITH GRILLED PINEAPPLE & SWEET-ONION SALSA

18 ounces fresh or frozen Alaskan wild salmon

1 tablespoon kosher salt

1 teaspoon freshly ground black pepper

½ cup dry white vermouth

3 tablespoons grapeseed or canola oil

1 medium Vidalia or other sweet onion, peeled and cut into ¼-inch slices

1 medium fresh pineapple, peeled, cored, and cut in half lengthwise

1 bunch of cilantro

Rinse and pat dry salmon. Trim off thin "belly" portion of fish, and grill separately, as it will cook faster. Cut remaining piece into two large or four smaller portions.

Place fish in non-reactive glass container, and season flesh with kosher salt and ground pepper to taste. Turn flesh side down, and add ½ cup of dry white vermouth. Cover and keep in refrigerator until about 20 minutes before grilling.

Preheat large stock pot to medium-high. Add 3 tablespoons of oil; then stir onions into pot, watching closely to prevent burning. Reduce heat to low, and sweat onion slices, uncovered, for 3 minutes. Turn heat up again to medium-high, and cook onions until they caramelize. Remove from heat, and set aside.

Preheat grill to high. Twenty minutes prior to grilling, remove salmon fillets from refrigerator and place on clean, waxed paper-covered platter to bring them to room temperature. (Cold fish will cook on the outside but remain raw on the inside.)

Reduce grill to medium-high; then place fish pieces on grill, surrounding them with pineapple sections. Close grill cover, and allow to cook for about 6 to 7 minutes. Use tongs to turn pineapple pieces so

Insert an instant-read thermometer into thickest portion of fish—it should read 130°F when cooked. Fish is done when flesh turns just opaque.

If the onions have cooled, reheat them in the microwave for about 30 seconds, or place on medium heat—don't let them burn!

Combine grilled pieces of pineapple with warmed onions. Using end of spatula, slice pineapple, allowing juice to combine with onion juices to create a delicious elixir.

Place fish on platter, and use metal spatula to remove the now crispy fish skin. Present fish fillets on platter, covered with grilled pineapple and caramelized sweet-onion salsa. Garnish platter with pieces of cilantro and crispy fish skin. ❈

fruit gets nice brown grill marks but does not burn. As fish pieces cook, turn them by inserting a metal spatula between fish flesh and skin. In one movement, invert fish back onto skin. Skin will continue to cook and get crispy and protect flesh from sticking to grates. Cover, and continue to cook for 2 to 3 minutes.

Remove the belly portion of salmon from the grill; set aside. Remove pineapple after it gets grill marks.

ASIAN SALMON BURGERS

1 pound salmon fillet, skin and pinbones removed, cut into 1-inch pieces

1 tablespoon fresh ginger, peeled and minced

1 tablespoon garlic, minced

2 green onions, including 2 inches of green tops, very thinly sliced

½ tablespoon fresh cilantro, chopped

1 teaspoon kosher or sea salt

1 tablespoon fresh lemon juice

½ tablespoon soy sauce

½ cup cracker meal

2 large eggs, lightly beaten

In a food processor fitted with a metal blade, pulse salmon just until coarsely ground, scraping down sides of work bowl once or twice. (Be careful; it's easy to go from chopped to mashed paste in seconds!)

Transfer salmon to a medium bowl. Add ginger, garlic, green onions, cilantro, salt, lemon juice, and soy sauce. Using a rubber spatula, mix to combine. Mix in cracker meal; add eggs. Dividing salmon mixture evenly; form into four 1-inch-thick patties. Refrigerate for at least 20 minutes before cooking. Patties can be prepared and refrigerated up to 8 hours ahead.

Preheat grill to medium. Place salmon burgers on grill, and cook for 4 to 5 minutes. Turn, and cook for an additional 4 to 5 minutes. ✳

NORTH AFRICAN-STYLE GRILLED SALMON

1 4-ounce jar green olives, drained and sliced

¾ cup low-fat plain yogurt

½ cup parsley, chopped

¼ cup cilantro, chopped

3 tablespoons lemon juice

2 tablespoons olive oil

1 tablespoon garlic, minced

2 teaspoons paprika

1 teaspoon ground cumin

1 teaspoon turmeric

½ teaspoon salt

¼ teaspoon red pepper flakes

4 salmon steaks or fillets, 4 to 6 ounces each, fresh, thawed, or frozen

1½ tablespoons olive or canola oil

1 teaspoon lemon-pepper seasoning

2 tablespoons slivered red onion

Reserve 2 tablespoons of the olives. Blend remaining olives, yogurt, parsley, cilantro, lemon juice, olive oil, garlic, paprika, cumin, turmeric, salt, and pepper flakes; set aside. Rinse any ice glaze from frozen salmon under cold water, and pat dry with a paper towel. Preheat grill to medium-high.

Coat a heavy skillet with oil, and place on grill to preheat. Brush both sides of salmon with oil. Place salmon in heated skillet, and cook, uncovered, about 3 to 4 minutes, until browned. Turn salmon over, and sprinkle with lemon pepper. Cover pan tightly, and reduce heat to medium. Cook an additional 6 to 8 minutes for frozen salmon; 3 to 4 minutes for fresh or thawed fish. To serve, spoon sauce over each salmon portion, and sprinkle with reserved olives and slivered onion. ❋

6

SEAFOOD

GRILLED COD, YAMS & PLAINTAIN SKEWERS WITH SPICY COCONUT SAUCE

4 to 6 wooden skewers

4 cod fillets, 4 to 6 ounces each

Olive oil, as needed

Sea salt, to taste

Pepper, to taste

1 jalapeño pepper, seeded and minced

3 cloves garlic, minced

2 large, ripe, black-skin plantains or large firm bananas, peeled and cut into 1-inch slices

2 medium yams or sweet potatoes, peeled and cut into 1½-inch chunks

4 tablespoons brown sugar, divided

½ teaspoon chili powder

⅛ teaspoon nutmeg

1 14-ounce can coconut milk (regular or lite)

⅔ cup fresh lime juice

4 small green onions, thinly sliced

1 tablespoon green Thai curry paste

2 tablespoons basil cut in thin strips

1 tablespoon cornstarch

¼ cup toasted coconut

Prior to grilling, soak wooden skewers in water for 30 minutes. Brush both sides of fish fillets with olive oil, and sprinkle with salt and pepper. Score top of fillets with cuts 1½ to 2 inches apart. Mix jalapeño pepper and garlic in a small bowl. Rub mixture into cod. Cover, and refrigerate.

In large a glass bowl, microwave plantains and yams for 4 to 5 minutes on high, just until vegetables begin to soften. In separate small bowl, blend 1 tablespoon salt, 2 tablespoons brown sugar, chili powder, and nutmeg. Pour 2 tablespoons of the olive oil over vegetables; sprinkle on brown sugar mixture; stir to coat. Thread vegetables onto skewers.

Preheat grill or broiler/oven to medium-high. In saucepan, blend coconut milk, lime juice, green onions, curry paste, 2 tablespoons brown sugar, basil, cornstarch, and 1 teaspoon salt until smooth. Cook on grill or stovetop until mixture boils and thickens, stirring frequently. Keep warm.

Place vegetable skewers on grill or broiling pan brushed with olive oil. Place cod fillets on grill rack brushed with olive oil. Cook cod and vegetable skewers 5 to 6 inches from heat for 6 to 8 minutes, turning skewers once during cooking. Cook just until fish is opaque throughout and vegetables are browned.

To serve, drizzle with ¼ cup sauce and 1 tablespoon toasted coconut. ❄

GRILLED TILAPIA WITH SUN-DRIED TOMATOES

1 teaspoon lemon juice

Salt and pepper to taste

1 teaspoon fresh cilantro, chopped

2 tilapia fillets (8 to 10 ounces each)

2 sun-dried tomatoes, julienned

1 medium tomato, diced

½ cup white wine

¼ red onion, diced

1 teaspoon fresh parsley, chopped

¼ cup light cream

Preheat grill to medium-low. Mix together lemon juice, salt, pepper, and cilantro. Pour over fish in a flat dish. In a medium saucepan, mix together all remaining ingredients except for cream. Bring to a boil; then add cream. Remove from heat. Grill tilapia 8 to 10 minutes, turning once. Place on plate; cover with sauce; and serve. ❊

GRILLED SWORDFISH WITH CITRUS SALSA

4 5-ounce swordfish steaks
1 tablespoon corn oil
Salt and pepper to taste

Prepare the citrus salsa—mix all ingredients except swordfish, corn oil, salt, and pepper, and let marinate for a couple of hours.

Season the swordfish steaks with salt and pepper to personal taste. Brush lightly with one tablespoon corn oil. Grill for about 5 minutes per side until fish is firm and slightly opaque. (Use a knife to check.)

Spoon the salsa over the charbroiled swordfish steaks. Garnish with mint sprigs. Great served with saffron rice, fresh asparagus, and baby carrots. ❄

CITRUS SALSA

1 ruby red grapefruit
½ orange, peeled
½ lime, peeled
1 lemon, peeled
1 medium red onion

1 cup red, green, and yellow
  bell pepper, diced
1 tablespoon cilantro, chopped
1 tablespoon mint, chopped
1 ounce tequila

Section and remove white membrane from grapefruit, orange, lime, and lemon; then cut each fruit into bite-size pieces. Finely dice onion. Mix together fruit, onion, peppers, cilantro, mint, and tequila. Let salsa marinate for 1 to 2 hours before serving.

GRILLED HALIBUT WITH A GREEN CHILI BLANKET

[*Recipe by Toni Bocci of Cordova, Arkansas*]

½ cup mayonnaise or plain, low-fat yogurt

1 4-ounce can mild green chilis, diced

1 tablespoon fresh lime juice

4 halibut steaks or fillets, fresh or frozen, 4 to 6 ounces each

1 12 x 18-inch sheet aluminum foil

1 tablespoon fresh cilantro or chives, chopped

Preheat grill to medium-high. Combine mayonnaise, green chilis, and lime juice; set aside.

Rinse any ice glaze from frozen halibut under cold water; pat dry with a paper towel. Place halibut on spray-coated foil sheet on grill. Cook 9 minutes for frozen halibut; 5 minutes for fresh or thawed fish.

Turn halibut over, and liberally spoon mayonnaise mixture onto cooked side of each portion. Sprinkle with cilantro, and cook an additional 5 to 10 minutes until fish is just opaque throughout. ❋

THAI-STYLE HALIBUT SKEWERS

2 tablespoons vegetable oil

1 tablespoon Thai green curry paste

1 tablespoon ginger, freshly grated

1 tablespoon rice wine vinegar

1 teaspoon nam pla (Thai fish sauce)

1 teaspoon toasted sesame oil

1½ pounds boneless, skinless halibut
  steaks or fillets, cut into 1½ inch pieces

12 fresh lemon grass stalks, each about
  ¼ inch thick and 6 inches long, or
  wood skewers, soaked for 30 minutes

Thoroughly blend oil, curry paste, ginger, vinegar, fish sauce, and sesame oil. Brush mixture on fish; cover; and refrigerate for 30 minutes.

Preheat grill to medium-high. Thread halibut onto skewers, two to three pieces per skewer. Place skewers on well-oiled grill. Grill halibut directly above heat source for 4 to 5 minutes per side, turning once during cooking. Cook just until fish is opaque throughout. ✻

CHARRED SUGAR-CRUSTED SALMON

**4 to 6 skinless salmon fillets
(4 to 6 ounces each)**

2 tablespoons canola oil

**¼ to ⅓ cup hot Chinese-style
or Dijon-style mustard,
if desired**

DRY SUGAR RUB

2 tablespoons sugar

1 tablespoon chili powder

1 teaspoon black pepper

½ tablespoon ground cumin

½ tablespoon paprika

½ tablespoon salt

¼ teaspoon dry mustard

Dash of cinnamon

Oil a cast-iron griddle, and preheat over grill or outdoor stovetop over medium-high heat. Blend all ingredients for dry sugar rub. Generously coat one side of each salmon fillet with rub.

Carefully place salmon fillets on griddle, seasoned side down. Cook about 2 minutes to sear; turn fillets over. Reduce heat to medium, and continue cooking 6 to 8 minutes. Cook just until fish is opaque throughout.

Serve salmon with mustard, if desired. ❊

4 Servings • Prep: 25 min. • Marinate: 30 min. • Grill: 7–10 min.

205

LEMON & GINGER GRILLED ALASKAN SALMON STRIPS

1½ pound Alaskan salmon fillet, skin on

¼ cup canola oil

¼ cup lemon juice

2 tablespoons soy sauce

2 tablespoons honey

½ teaspoon ground ginger

¼ cup green onion, chopped

1 teaspoon lemon peel

Cut salmon fillet into 1¼-inch strips. Mix canola oil, lemon juice, soy sauce, honey, ginger, green onion, and lemon peel together in a large, shallow glass dish. Add salmon strips, and coat well. Marinate 30 minutes, turning several times. Preheat grill to medium-high. Remove salmon strips from marinade; discard marinade.

Place salmon, skin side up, on grill for 3 minutes. Turn carefully, and continue to cook, skin side down, for an additional 3 to 4 minutes, or until just done and center flakes with fork. To remove strips from grill, run spatula between skin and salmon. This will provide a plate-ready, skinless strip. Garnish dish with chopped green onion, lemon peel, and lemon slices. ❋

6

SEAFOOD

ZOE'S GRILLED SALMON & PINEAPPLE SALSA ON TOASTED CIABATTA TRIANGLES

6 salmon fillets, 6 to 8 ounces each

3 large lemons

2 large limes

8 ounces sour cream

Cooking oil spray

6 12-inch squares of heavy-duty aluminum foil

1 tablespoon fresh cilantro, chopped

1 large ciabatta bread

Rinse salmon in cool water, and pat dry. Remove any pinbones.

Slice one lemon and one lime into six slices each. Add grated zest and juice from one lime to sour cream; set aside.

Spray the skin side of each fillet, and place one fillet in each sheet of foil. Season with salt and pepper; then top with fresh cilantro and one slice each of the lemon and lime. Squeeze lemon juice over fish; seal edges of foil.

Preheat grill to medium. Place foil packets on grill, and cook for 5 to 8 minutes. While salmon is cooking, cut ciabatta into three triangles, and then in half to create six portions. Toast on grill.

Spoon salsa over toasted ciabatta triangles. Drizzle with olive oil; place cooked salmon on top; then add a dollop of the sour cream. ❋

This recipe is for individual portions; however, you can modify it to prepare the whole side of the fish—loosely enclosing it in an aluminum foil "envelope." Use the recipe as a guideline, and adopt at will to suit your own taste.—CB

PINEAPPLE SALSA

3 medium tomatoes, diced

1 large onion, finely chopped

¼ fresh pineapple, cut into chunks

1 clove garlic, minced

1 bunch of cilantro, chopped

Olive oil

Chili flakes

Salt and pepper

Combine tomatoes, onion, pineapple chunks, garlic, and cilantro in medium bowl. Season with salt, pepper, olive oil, and chili flakes to taste.

6

SEAFOOD

HERBED WHOLE SALMON ON THE GRILL

1 whole salmon or large salmon fillet, fresh, thawed, or frozen

4 sheets heavy-duty aluminum foil, 6 inches larger than length of salmon

1 large onion, sliced, or 2 leeks, separated into leaves

1 lemon or lime, halved

1 tablespoon preferred seasoning mix

1½ cups fresh herbs, coarsely chopped (See suggested combinations of seasonings and herbs, above right.)

SUGGESTED FLAVOR COMBINATIONS

Mexican—lime, cilantro, onion, Mexican seasoning

Mediterranean—lemon, oregano, basil, Italian seasoning

Continental—lemon, dill, leeks, lemon-pepper seasoning

Cajun—lemon, onion, celery salt, Cajun seasoning.

Rinse any ice glaze from frozen salmon under cold water, and pat dry with paper towels. Lay out two sheets of aluminum foil, double thickness, on large tray. Spray top layer with cooking spray.

Lay half of the onions or leeks lengthwise in center of the foil. Place salmon on top of onions; then squeeze lemon or lime on both sides of fish. Sprinkle dry seasoning on both sides of salmon. Place fresh herbs over, under, and—if fish is not frozen—inside the belly cavity of fish.

Lay out remaining two sheets of foil, double thickness. Spray top sheet with oil; then place, coated side down, over salmon. Roll up, crimp, and seal all sides of foil to form a packet.

Cook salmon over medium-hot grill, 5 to 6 inches from heat, for 50 to 60 minutes if frozen; 45 to 55 minutes if fresh or thawed, turning packet every 15 minutes. Cook just until fish is opaque throughout. ✻

6

SEAFOOD

CB'S FAMOUS SMOKED SALMON

1 3- to 5-pound side of salmon, filleted, 1 inch at thickest part and 12 inches long

2 cups brown sugar

½ cup pickling salt

1 3-ounce bag crab-boil seasoning

1 tablespoon blackstrap molasses

> *Salmon is high in beneficial oils, low in saturated fat and cholesterol, and easy to prepare in so many ways. This recipe produces a moist fish that makes an impressive hors d'oeuvre or appetizer. Note the 8-hour curing time.* —CB

Ask your fishmonger to remove pinbones from the salmon. Trim thin parts of the fillet—last 3 inches of the tail and belly area. (You can scramble them with eggs for breakfast.) Rinse the fillet under cold running water, and pat dry using paper towels.

Combine brown sugar, pickling salt, and contents of crab-boil bag into a bowl, and mix well. Add enough water to these dry ingredients to form a slurry that is slightly wetter in texture than paste. Place salmon fillet in a large, 2-inch-deep dish or large plastic food bag, and coat the flesh with slurry. Cover dish tightly with plastic wrap or the seal bag, and refrigerate overnight. Two hours before smoking the fish, remove from refrigerator. Scrape off the slurry mixture, and place salmon into a wire strainer to drain and to save small bits of the crab boil.

Place salmon fillet flesh side up on a baking sheet; pat dry. (Do not rinse.) Spread remaining bits of crab boil over the fish. Carefully crisscross salmon with a very thin line of blackstrap molasses on top of the spice bits.

Allow toppings on fish to dry, using a hair dryer on low setting to speed up the process. Toppings on fish are dry when they are "tacky" to the touch.

Set your smoker for 250°F. You can add alder or cherry wood chips for extra flavor. A wet smoker is preferable for this fish; but if you're using a dry smoker, keep a bowl of water in the smoker to preserve the moist texture of the fish. Make certain the grill grates are clean of all debris.

Using your hands, place the fish flesh side down and across the grates, so that marks run from side to side on the flesh. Close the smoker lid. Maintaining an even temperature, smoke the salmon for 1 to 2 hours—depending upon the heat of the smoke, the number of fillets, and the thickness of the fish. When fish is done, use heat-resistant gloves to remove the grate from the smoker with the fish still on it. Placing a large baking pan over the fish, turn the grate over so that the baking sheet is on the bottom. Remove the grates. Refrigerate the fish until serving time. Serve with dark bread, sliced red onions, cream cheese, lemon wedges, and capers. ✳

6

SEAFOOD

7 Vegetables, Sides & Salads

(Left) Original Oklahoma BBQ Beans, page 227

UNCLE JIM'S TIME-TESTED GRILLED CORN

4 ears corn, still in husk

Olive oil for brushing

**Garlic or onion, chopped and
    caramelized**

Fresh herbs

Nutmeg

Sea salt

Black pepper

Pull back on each corn husk, but do not remove it. Remove and discard corn silk; then soak the cobs in a pot of cold water for 15 minutes. Preheat the grill to medium. Remove the corn from the water, and brush the kernels with olive oil. Spread corn with the caramelized garlic or onion, fresh herbs, nutmeg, sea salt, and black pepper. Tie the husks back in place with twine. Place the prepared ears of corn over direct heat on the grill, turning every few minutes to create grill marks. Finish the corn with indirect heat on the top shelf of the grill with the cover closed. Allow the corn to roast for another 15 minutes. 🌽

ASIAN SUPER SLAW

This colorful, Asian-inspired salad is great with grilled ribs, chicken, or pork chops.

6 tablespoons rice vinegar

6 tablespoons vegetable oil

5 tablespoons creamy peanut butter

3 tablespoons soy sauce

3 tablespoons golden brown sugar, packed

2 tablespoons fresh ginger, minced and peeled

1½ tablespoons garlic, minced

5 cups green cabbage, thinly sliced

2 cups red cabbage, thinly sliced

2 large red or yellow bell peppers, cut into matchstick-size strips

2 medium carrots, peeled and cut into matchstick-size strips

8 large scallions, cut into matchstick-size strips

½ cup fresh cilantro, chopped

Whisk together the first seven ingredients in a small bowl to blend. Cover, and let chill. (The dressing can be made 1 day ahead.) Let the dressing stand at room temperature for 30 minutes before continuing.

Combine the remaining ingredients in a large bowl. Add the dressing, and toss to coat. Season the salad with salt and pepper, and serve.

7

VEGETABLES, SIDES & SALADS

MEXICAN POTATO SALAD

3 medium fresh green chilies

2 pounds red potatoes, peels on, cut into wedges

6 medium tomatillos, husked and cut into ½-inch pieces

1¼ cups scallions, chopped

¼ cup fresh cilantro, chopped

1 cup sour cream

3 tablespoons fresh lime juice

2 teaspoons ground cumin

Salt and freshly ground pepper to taste

[*Perfect with grilled flank steak or Southwestern-style chicken.*]

Preheat grill to high. Grill the chilies until blackened on all sides. Enclose chilies in a paper bag, and let them rest for 10 minutes. Peel, seed, and chop the chilies; transfer them to a large bowl.

Steam the potatoes until just tender, about 10 minutes. Cool, and combine them with the chilies. Mix in the tomatillos, scallions, and cilantro.

Whisk together the sour cream, lime juice, and cumin in a small bowl. Pour the mixture over the potatoes and chilies; then gently toss just to coat potatoes. Season with salt and pepper. Cover, and refrigerate for 4 to 6 hours to blend the flavors. Let salad stand at room temperature for 30 minutes before serving. 🍎

Tomatillos are green, tomato-like vegetables with thin, paper-like husks. They are available at Latin American markets and some supermarkets. If you can't find them, substitute green or yellow tomatoes.

7

VEGETABLES, SIDES & SALADS

GRILLED CORN WITH SUN-DRIED TOMATO PESTO

4 ears of corn in husks
½ cup sun-dried tomatoes
2 tablespoons whole pine nuts
¼ cup olive oil
1 teaspoon garlic, chopped
Salt and pepper to taste

Soak the corn in water for 45 minutes to 1 hour. Place the remaining ingredients in a blender; puree until smooth.

Preheat grill to medium. Remove the corn from the water. Peel back the husks, leaving them attached at the stem. Grill the corn for 8 to 10 minutes, turning often. Remove from the grill, and spread the corn with the sun-dried pesto. Serve immediately. 🌶

MARY'S TOMATO, CUCUMBER & GARLIC SALAD

1 large garlic clove, chopped

1 teaspoon kosher salt

1 cup vegetable oil

⅛ cup red wine vinegar

Juice of ½ lemon

1 large ripe tomato, seeded and chopped into bite-size pieces

1 long, thin cucumber, thinly sliced

1 head iceberg lettuce, torn into pieces

Large wooden salad bowl

[*This salad is perfect with steak or grilled pork chops.*]

Put the chopped garlic into a salad bowl. Pour the salt on top of the garlic. Using a fork, mash the salt into the garlic against the side of a wooden bowl until a paste is formed. Pour in the oil, vinegar, and lemon juice, and whisk with a fork until well blended. Add the chopped tomato, and let it marinate for several minutes. Add the cucumber, and let it marinate for several more minutes. (This allows the vegetables to absorb the flavor of the dressing.) Just before serving, add lettuce. Toss and serve immediately.

Quick Dish • 6 Servings • Prep: 10 min. • Grill: 1–2 min. • Broil: 2 min.

221

GRILLED ENDIVE WITH BLUE CHEESE

6 heads endive

4½ tablespoons olive oil

Salt and pepper to taste

6 ounces blue cheese, crumbled

2 tablespoons balsamic vinegar

2 tablespoons fresh parsley, chopped

Heat the grill to medium-high, and preheat the broiler. Cut each endive lengthwise into two sections, and place in a single layer on a baking sheet. Brush the endive with 4 tablespoons of oil; then sprinkle with salt and pepper. Grill until crisp-tender, about 1 minute per side. Return endive to the baking sheet. Sprinkle with cheese. Broil until the cheese melts and bubbles, about 2 minutes. Transfer the endive-cheese combination to a platter. Drizzle with ½ tablespoon oil and the balsamic vinegar. Top with parsley. Serve immediately. 🌶

7

VEGETABLES, SIDES & SALADS

GRILLED BREAD & TOMATO SALAD

¼ cup butter, melted

1 tablespoon garlic, chopped

½ loaf day-old French bread, cut into 1-inch slices

5 tomatoes, seeded and cut into chunks

½ red onion, finely chopped

¼ cup extra-virgin olive oil

¼ cup balsamic vinegar

1 tablespoons Italian parsley, coarsely chopped

1 tablespoons fresh basil leaves, coarsely chopped

Salt and pepper to taste

Preheat the grill to medium-high. Melt the butter in a small saucepan; then add the chopped garlic. Brush the garlic butter on both sides of the bread slices. Grill the bread over medium-high heat until lightly browned, 3 to 4 minutes for each side.

Cut the grilled bread slices into quarters, and place them in a large salad bowl. Add the chopped tomato and red onion. Drizzle the olive oil and balsamic vinegar over the salad. Sprinkle with salt, pepper, parsley, and basil. Toss well. Let the salad stand about 30 minutes to allow the bread to absorb liquids. Serve at room temperature. 🍎

4–6 Servings • Prep: 30 min. • Marinate: 2 hr. • Bake: 20 min. Chill: 2 hr.

223

LAYERED CORN-BREAD SALAD

CORN BREAD

1 tablespoon vegetable oil

3 cups buttermilk

2 eggs

2 cups yellow cornmeal

1 teaspoon baking soda

1 teaspoon baking powder

1 teaspoon salt

½ cup jalapeño peppers, chopped.

Preheat the oven to 450°F. Coat the bottom and sides of a 10-inch iron skillet with vegetable oil, and heat it in the oven. In a medium bowl, combine the buttermilk and eggs; stir. Add the cornmeal, baking soda, baking powder, salt, and jalapeño peppers, continuing to stir briskly. Pour the batter into the hot skillet. Bake for 20 minutes or until lightly browned.

DRESSING

1 package ranch-style dressing mix

8 ounces sour cream

1 cup mayonnaise

1 pan corn bread (from recipe), crumbled

2 16-ounce cans pinto beans, drained

3 cups cheddar cheese, shredded

3 large tomatoes, chopped

½ cup green bell pepper, chopped

½ cup green onions, chopped

½ cup chili peppers, chopped

1½ cups bacon pieces

1 15-ounce can
   corn, drained

Combine the dressing mix, sour cream, and mayonnaise; set aside. Place half of the crumbled corn bread in the bottom of a large serving bowl. Top with 1 can of pinto beans. Follow this with half of the cheese, tomatoes, bell peppers, green onions, chili peppers, bacon, corn, and dressing mixture. Repeat this process, ending with the dressing mixture. Cover and chill mixture for at least 2 hours before serving. ❦

7

VEGETABLES, SIDES & SALADS

GRILLED POLENTA

3 cups water

1 teaspoon salt

2 tablespoons unsalted butter

¾ cup polenta or coarse-ground
    yellow cornmeal

¾ cup Parmesan
    cheese, freshly grated

¼ teaspoons cayenne pepper

Olive oil

[*Great with grilled chicken breast, steaks, and chops.*]

Combine the water, salt, and butter in a saucepan, and bring to a boil. Gradually add the polenta, whisking constantly to avoid lumps. Reduce heat, and continue cooking, stirring constantly, until mixture is very thick, 10 to 15 minutes. Remove the pan from the heat, and stir in Parmesan cheese and cayenne pepper.

Line a 9-inch pie plate with plastic wrap, letting it extend over the edges. Spread the polenta evenly over plastic wrap, and smooth the top. Cover tightly with plastic wrap, and chill until firm, at least 1 hour.

Preheat the grill to medium. Invert the pie plate to allow molded polenta to be removed. Peel off the plastic wrap. Cut the polenta into six wedges. Brush each wedge lightly on both sides with oil. Arrange the polenta wedges on the cooking grate. Grill, turning 2 or 3 times, until golden, about 10 minutes. ❧

BECKY'S BARLEY CASSEROLE

½ cup Marsala wine

2 cups chicken broth

1 cup pearl barley

1 tablespoon butter

1 medium onion, chopped

1 4-ounce can whole button
mushrooms, drained

¼ teaspoon dried rosemary

⅛ teaspoon freshly ground
black pepper

1 tablespoon fresh parsley,
chopped

[*Rebecca Anderson, a "Sizzle on the Grill" reader from Melissa, Texas, makes this fuss-free dish during the holiday season. I think it's the perfect accompaniment to Thanksgiving turkey cooked in The Big Easy.* —CB]

Preheat the oven to 350°F. Combine the wine and broth in a 2-quart microwave- and oven-safe casserole dish. Microwave on high until the mixture boils, about 4 to 5 minutes. Stir in the barley, butter, onion, mushrooms, rosemary, and pepper. Cover the dish tightly, and bake for approximately 1 hour or until the liquid is absorbed and the barley is tender. Fluff the barley with a fork, and garnish it with chopped parsley. Serve warm.

GRILLED CORN & BLACK BEAN SALAD

2 ears corn, grilled

1 cup cooked black beans, drained and rinsed, if canned

1 small red bell pepper, peeled, cored, and seeded

3 tablespoons fresh lemon juice

1 garlic clove, minced

2 tablespoons fresh cilantro, chopped

2 teaspoons fresh tarragon, chopped

Salt and freshly ground pepper to taste

3 tablespoons olive oil

Using a sharp knife, cut the corn kernels from the cob. In a large bowl, combine the black beans, corn, and bell pepper. In a small bowl, whisk together the lemon juice, garlic, herbs, salt, and pepper. Add the olive oil, blending well. Pour the dressing mixture over the corn and black bean salad, tossing well. Serve at room temperature or chilled.

ORIGINAL OKLAHOMA BBQ BEANS

2 pounds dry pinto beans

1 tablespoon salt

1 whole onion, peeled and split through (secure with 2 wooden picks to hold together)

2 large cloves garlic, with wooden toothpick inserted into each

¼ pound salt pork, slab bacon, or smoked jaw

⅓ cup shortening

2 cups onions, very finely minced

½ cup all-purpose flour

2 cups tomato juice (or ¾ cup tomato sauce, or ⅓ cup tomato paste diluted to make 2 cups)

Salt and pepper to taste

¼ cup firmly packed brown sugar

¼ cup molasses

Hot pepper sauce to taste

Soak the beans overnight in 2 quarts water. Discard the water, and rinse the beans thoroughly. Transfer to a large pot and fill with water to 1 inch above surface of beans. Add salt, whole onion, garlic cloves, and salt pork. Cover, and simmer over medium heat until beans are tender, not mushy. Remove from heat.

In saucepan, heat shortening and minced onion over high heat. Sauté until onions are translucent. Add flour, and stir until mixture turns golden. Remove from heat, and add tomato juice, salt, and pepper. Stir until lump-free. Discard whole onion and garlic from beans. Ladle some beans into sauce; then stir sauce back into bean pot. Stir in brown sugar and molasses. Remove salt pork and discard, or cut into small pieces about size of beans, and stir in pork. Add the hot pepper sauce. Bring the mixture to a boil, stirring; then remove from the heat.

Let beans stand for at least 1 hour before serving. 🦎

GEORGE JV'S RANCH BEANS

1 pound ground beef
1 package dry onion soup mix
½ cup water
1 cup ketchup
2 tablespoons prepared mustard
2 tablespoons vinegar
1 can (11-ounce) pork and beans
1 can (28-ounce) baked beans
1 small can lima beans (optional)

Preheat the oven to 400°F. Brown the ground beef in a large skillet. Stir in the remaining ingredients, and pour the mixture into a 2-quart casserole dish. Bake for 30 minutes. 🐛

CB'S HONEY-BUTTER SWEET POTATOES

6 medium sweet potatoes
¼ cup honey
¼ cup unsalted butter

Preheat the grill to medium. Cut the sweet potatoes into ½-inch slices, and place them on grill. Mix the honey into the softened butter. After the sweet potato slices have grilled for 8 to 10 minutes, spread them with the honey-butter mixture, and turn them. Grill the slices for 8 minutes more; then turn them, and spread on more honey butter. Continue grilling until the honey butter is bubbling and the sweet potato slices are tender. Serve hot or warm.

SMOKED GOUDA SWEET POTATOES WITH PRALINE-PECAN CRUMBLE

4 tablespoons butter, divided

2½ pounds sweet potatoes, peeled and cut into ¾-inch cubes

½ teaspoon salt

1 teaspoon Creole seasoning

8 ounces smoked Gouda, shredded

1½ cups cranberry juice

½ cup dark brown sugar

3 tablespoon flour

½ cup pecans, chopped

⅛ teaspoon nutmeg

This sweet and savory recipe, submitted by Judy Armstrong of Prairieville, Louisiana, has a short list of special holiday ingredients, is quick to assemble, and complements the flavors of fried, grilled, or smoked turkey.

Preheat the oven to 375°F. Spread 1 tablespoon of butter over the bottom and sides of a 9 x 12-inch baking dish.

Layer the cubed sweet potatoes in the baking dish, and toss them with the salt, Creole seasoning, and smoked Gouda. Pour cranberry juice over the mixture. Cover the dish, and bake for 30 minutes.

In the meantime, melt the remaining butter in a saucepan over low heat. Stir in the brown sugar, flour, pecans, and nutmeg. Mix well, and set it aside until the potatoes and cheese finish baking.

Remove the casserole from the oven, and spoon the pecan mixture over top. Continue baking, uncovered, for an additional 30 minutes. ✤

SPICY GRILLED FRIES

1 tablespoon paprika

1 teaspoon freshly ground
black pepper

1 teaspoon kosher salt

½ teaspoon chili powder

Pinch of cayenne (optional)

4 large russet or baking
potatoes, scrubbed but
not peeled

Olive oil

Preheat the grill to medium-low. Combine the first five ingredients in a small bowl. Cut the potatoes in half lengthwise; then slice each half into long wedges that are about ½ inch thick in the middle. Place the potatoes in a large plastic storage bag, and pour the oil on top. Shake well to coat; then sprinkle the potatoes generously with the spice mixture, and shake again until they are well coated. Place the potatoes directly on the grate, and grill for 30 to 35 minutes, turning every 5 to 7 minutes. Dab them lightly with additional oil as needed. The potatoes are ready when crisp and golden brown outside and soft in the middle. 🌶

ROASTED-GARLIC MASHED POTATOES

4 Russet potatoes

1 cup milk

½ cup buttermilk

¼ cup unsalted butter

2 heads of roasted garlic
   (See page 289.)

¼ cup extra-virgin olive oil

1 tablespoon dried thyme

Salt and pepper to taste

Peel potatoes, and cut them into quarters. Boil them in salted water for 20 to 30 minutes or until tender. Meanwhile, heat the milk, buttermilk, and butter in a pot. When the potatoes are done, drain and return them to the same pot. Squeeze the garlic cloves out of their skins; then add the milk and butter a little at a time; mash potatoes until the desired consistency is achieved. Season the potatoes with salt and pepper to taste. Serve hot.

DOUBLE-GRILLED STUFFED POTATOES

6 large baking potatoes
Stuffing mixture (See opposite page.)

[*Serve these hearty potatoes as a main dish with salad or as a side dish.*]

Preheat the grill to high. Wash the potatoes; pierce them with a fork; and wrap them in aluminum foil. Grill for 45 minutes or until the potatoes test done. Allow them to cool slightly.

Unwrap the potatoes. Cut each in half lengthwise. Carefully scoop the potato out of each half to within ¼ inch of skin, reserving the skins. Add potatoes to stuffing mixture. Spoon the mixture into the reserved potato skins. Sprinkle the remaining cheese and finely diced bell peppers over the potatoes. Return them to the grill, and cook them over medium heat until the cheese melts.

Note: potatoes can be prepared ahead of time and returned to the grill or oven just before serving. ❧

STUFFING MIXTURE

1 16-ounce carton sour cream

1½ cups cheddar cheese, shredded
  and divided

1 stick butter, softened

2 teaspoons salt

Pepper to taste

1 pound barbecue pork butt,
  finely-chopped

1 each large red, yellow, and green
  bell pepper, finely diced

Place the hot potatoes in a large
mixing bowl. Add the sour cream,
¾ cup of cheese, and butter, blending well. Stir in the salt, pepper,
and finely chopped barbecue.

GRILLED RED POTATOES & GREEN BEANS WITH PESTO

2 cups water

1 pound fresh green beans, rinsed and trimmed

12 red potatoes (about 1½ pounds)

Nonstick vegetable oil spray

2½ cups basil leaves

¼ cup Italian parsley, chopped

2 tablespoons olive oil

⅓ cup vegetable broth

2 large garlic cloves, peeled and halved

¼ cup pine nuts

¼ cup Parmesan cheese, grated

Steam beans in microwave or steamer basket on stovetop until almost tender, about 8 minutes. Transfer beans to bowl of ice water to stop cooking. Drain beans, and cut them in half.

Preheat grill. Thread three red potatoes onto each of four skewers. Spray the potatoes and grill with oil. Place skewers on grill. Turning as needed, grill 20 to 30 minutes or until potatoes are tender. Remove potatoes from grill; set aside. When cool enough to handle, remove potatoes from skewers, and cut each potato in half. Set aside.

To make pesto, combine basil, parsley, olive oil, broth, garlic, pine nuts, and Parmesan in a food processor or blender. Blend until ingredients resemble a sauce. Transfer to a bowl.

While grill is still hot, place wire basket on grill; lightly oil basket; and then add potatoes and beans. Place basket on grill, and heat, tossing frequently, 4 to 5 minutes. Remove from grill, and divide mixture among four plates. Serve with pesto. ❦

MUSHROOM-STUFFED POTATOES

4 large baking potatoes

Salt and freshly ground black pepper
   to taste

4 tablespoons butter

1 tablespoons green onions, minced

1 clove garlic, minced

8 ounces fresh mushrooms, sliced

¼ cup heavy cream

1 tablespoons fresh chives, minced

1 tablespoons fresh parsley, minced

¼ cup Swiss or Gouda Cheese, grated

Preheat the grill to high. Wash the potatoes; pierce them with a fork; and wrap them in aluminum foil. Grill for 45 minutes or until the potatoes test done. Allow them to cool slightly. Unwrap the potatoes. Slice the top off each one, cutting horizontally. Carefully scoop out the potato pulp to within ¼ inch of skin, reserving the skins. Season the potato shell with salt and pepper. Place the hot potatoes in a large mixing bowl.

In a medium saucepan, melt the butter, and sauté the onions and garlic for 1 minute over medium-high heat. Add the mushrooms, and sauté until tender. Add the cream; cook and stir the mixture over medium heat until well blended. Remove from the heat, and add the chives and parsley. Pour the mushroom sauce onto the potato pulp, and fold them together. Spoon the stuffing into the potato shells, and top with cheese. Place the shells on a baking sheet, and heat them in the oven at 350°F for 20 minutes or until potatoes are warm and the cheese is brown and bubbling. 🍏

7

VEGETABLES, SIDES & SALADS

INDIAN SPICE-GRILLED CAULIFLOWER

4 tablespoons butter

¼ teaspoon cinnamon

¼ teaspoon dried coriander

½ teaspoon fresh ginger, grated

⅛ teaspoon saffron threads, crushed (optional)

¼ teaspoons ground cardamom

1 tablespoon garlic, minced

1 head cauliflower, cut into florets

In a skillet, cook the butter over medium heat until golden brown. Combine the cinnamon, coriander, ginger, saffron, cardamom, and garlic; stir this mixture into the butter. Add the cauliflower, stirring to coat the florets with sauce, and cook for 3 to 4 minutes, stirring occasionally. Transfer the cauliflower florets to a grill basket, saving any remaining sauce for basting. Grill the vegetables over high heat, basting and turning them frequently. Cook for 5 minutes or until they are crunchy-tender. Be careful not to overcook. Serve. 🌶

BUTTERY BOURBON SCALLIONS

24 scallions, washed, trimmed, and peeled

⅓ cup bourbon

1 tablespoon butter

1 teaspoon brown sugar

Salt and freshly ground pepper to taste

[*Great with fish or chicken.*]

Place the scallions in a large bowl. Combine the bourbon, butter, and sugar in a saucepan. Place over medium heat, and cook just long enough to melt the butter and dissolve the sugar. Pour the mixture over the scallions; toss well.

Cut two squares of aluminum foil, stacking them to make them double the thickness. Transfer the scallions and sauce onto the foil, making sure to get all remaining sauce out of the bowl. Wrap the foil around the scallions, leaving sides high enough to contain the sauce, and seal them at the top.

Preheat the grill. Place the foiled scallions on the grill, away from direct heat. Close the lid, and grill for 30 to 40 minutes, stirring several times to make sure the scallions don't char. ❧

7

VEGETABLES, SIDES & SALADS

GRILLED GREEN BEANS WITH WALNUTS

¾ **pound green beans, trimmed**

2 **teaspoons olive oil**

¼ **cup walnuts, toasted and finely chopped**

2 **teaspoons walnut oil**

2 **teaspoons fresh lemon juice**

Freshly ground pepper

Toss the beans with oil, and grill them for 5 to 8 minutes in an oiled grill basket until tender. Remove beans, and toss with walnuts, walnut oil, and lemon juice. Season the beans with pepper, and serve immediately. 🐝

GARLIC-GRILLED PORTABELLAS

4 Portabella mushrooms, about 1 pound

⅓ cup extra-virgin olive oil

3 tablespoons lemon juice

2 cloves garlic, peeled and minced

Salt and pepper to taste

2 tablespoons fresh parsley, minced

Preheat the grill to medium-high. Brush any dirt or grit off the mushrooms with a damp paper towel. Remove the stems. Combine the oil, lemon juice, and garlic in a bowl. Brush the caps on both sides with the garlic oil; sprinkle salt and pepper on both sides, and let them stand for 15 minutes, stem side up. Place the caps on a well-oiled grill, stem side up; grill them for 3 to 4 minutes. Turn the caps over, and grill them for another 3 to 4 minutes or until easily pierced with a knife. Do not burn or overcook them; the centers should be tender and moist. Transfer the caps to a platter, and cut them into thick slices. Garnish with parsley before serving. ❦

CB'S GRILLED ARTICHOKES

2 large, fresh artichokes
1 tablespoon kosher salt or sea salt
2 tablespoons olive oil
Freshly ground black pepper

[*A CB-and-son recipe from "Sizzle on Grill" for Father's Day 2006*]

Using kitchen shears, trim the tips of the artichoke leaves about ½ inch down. Rinse or spray artichokes with water, taking care to remove any dirt or debris between the leaves. Place the artichokes on a cutting surface. Using a sharp knife, slice them in half to expose the heart and "choke."

Steam the artichokes in a pot on the range until tender, about 10 to 15 minutes. Remove from pot, and chill in an ice-water bath until cool to touch. (Hint: use previously cooked artichokes stored overnight in a cooler.)

Preheat the grill to low. Using a teaspoon, carve away the choke, making sure to leave the heart. You can cut these halves once more to create quarters if you prefer. Drizzle the artichokes with olive oil, and season them with salt and pepper. Grill cut side down—checking or turning side-to-side every few minutes—until grill marks begin to show. Remove, and serve artichokes as a side dish or appetizer.

We like to season ready-made mayonnaise with tarragon, parsley, and lemon zest for dipping. ▪

CHINESE-STYLE VEGETABLES

1 head baby bok choy
1 head napa cabbage
⅛ cup olive oil
⅛ cup chicken broth

Preheat the grill to medium. Separate the bok choy and cabbage leaves, and rinse them thoroughly; then dry the leaves with paper towels. Mix the olive oil and chicken broth, and sprinkle the mixture onto the vegetable leaves. Put vegetables into a grill wok or basket, and grill, basting with the oil and broth mixture, until the leaves are just tender. ❧

MARIAN'S HOMEMADE TOMATO PICKLE

2 pounds tomatoes

1 green pepper

3 red peppers

1 large eggplant

1 pound onions,
   peeled and finely
   chopped

4 large cloves garlic,
   crushed

14 ounces sugar

½ pint malt vinegar

1 tablespoon salt

2 tablespoons paprika

1 6-ounce can
   tomato puree

Peel the tomatoes; place them in boiling water for a few seconds; drain; and place them in ice water. The skins will come off easily. Chop the tomatoes; then seed, clean, and chop the peppers and eggplant. Put vegetables in a large, heavy pan with the onions and garlic; bring it to a boil. Cover the pan with a lid, and simmer for about 1 hour, stirring occasionally, until the veggies are tender.

Add the sugar, vinegar, salt, and paprika to the pot, and bring to a boil over medium heat, stirring until the sugar has dissolved. Continue to cook the mixture for 20 minutes until it achieves the consistency of chutney, keeping constant watch at the end of the cooking time to make sure the pickle does not burn on the bottom of the pan.

Spoon the pickle into sterilized canning jars, and top them with a waxed-paper cutout; then place a lid on the jars. Leave them to cool overnight, and retighten the lid on each jar in the morning. Place the jars in a dark, cool place for at least 4 weeks to mature the flavors. ❧

Marian is a regular reader of "Sizzle on Grill." She prepares this mild relish each year for her friends and family to enjoy. Her advice: "It takes a while to make this pickle, so I make enough for 12 months of use. It goes well with ham, cheese, and sausages."—CB

CARROTS WITH SNAP

32 baby carrots or 8 regular carrots,
    cut into 2-inch pieces
½ jalapeño pepper, seeded
    and chopped
¼ teaspoon unsalted butter
Salt and black pepper to taste

Place eight baby carrots each on four pieces of heavy-duty foil. Add the chopped pepper and butter to each; then add salt and pepper to taste. Fold up the edges of each piece of foil to create a tight seal to form packets. Grill the packets over medium heat, turning once, for 20 to 25 minutes. 🍎

SPINACH-STUFFED VIDALIA ONIONS

6 medium Vidalia or other sweet onions

1 pound fresh spinach

2 teaspoons butter, melted

¼ cup cream

1 teaspoon Worcestershire sauce

Salt and freshly ground pepper to taste

Dash of cayenne pepper

Parmesan cheese, grated

Preheat the grill to medium. Peel the onions, and place them in a steamer rack over simmering water. Steam them until they begin to soften, yet are still firm, about 5 minutes. Remove them from the heat. Wash the spinach, and remove the stems. Pour the water from the onions over the spinach in the colander. Drain the spinach well, squeezing with your hands, and place on a paper towel to drain. Chop the spinach finely. Sauté it in melted butter; add the cream and Worcestershire; and season with salt and pepper.

Hollow the onions, and fill them with the spinach mixture. Sprinkle onions with cayenne pepper and Parmesan cheese. Wrap the stuffed onions in foil, and grill them for about 20 minutes.

6 Servings • Prep: 10 min. • Marinate: 4–6 hr. • Grill: 20–25 min.

247

GRILLED ZUCCHINI PARMESAN

3 zucchini or yellow squash, sliced

2 tomatoes, diced

½ teaspoon oregano

Salt and pepper to taste

3 tablespoons Parmesan cheese, grated

3 tablespoons butter, melted

Preheat the grill to medium-high. Place the zucchini and tomatoes on six squares of aluminum foil. Sprinkle the seasoning on top of each. Top with butter. Seal the foil lightly, and grill for 20 to 25 minutes, turning every 10 minutes. Remove the foiled vegetables from the grill; unwrap them; and sprinkle them with Parmesan cheese. 🍎

7

VEGETABLES, SIDES & SALADS

OUTSTANDING ONION RINGS

1 giant-size sweet onion
1½ cups flour
1 teaspoon salt
¼ teaspoon freshly ground black pepper
⅛ teaspoons cayenne pepper
1½ cups buttermilk
Vegetable oil for frying
Popcorn salt, to taste

Peel the onion, removing the tough outer layer of the onion with the skin. Cut into horizontal slices about ½ inch thick. Separate the slices into individual rings.

Combine the flour, salt, black pepper, and cayenne in a shallow bowl; stir to mix. Pour the buttermilk into a separate bowl. Coat the onion rings, a few at a time, in the flour mixture, shaking off the excess, and place them in a baking dish. One or two at a time, dip the onion rings into buttermilk. Remove, and coat them again in the flour mixture, shaking off any excess. Transfer the rings back to the baking dish. Repeat the process with all the remaining onion rings.

Pour the oil to a depth of ½ to 1 inch in a cast-iron skillet or deep fryer, and heat over medium-high heat. When the temperature reaches 375°F, add onion rings a few at time. Allow enough room for each of the onion rings to fry without touching one another. Cook, turning once, until deep golden brown on both sides, about 3 minutes. Remove the onion rings from the oil, and drain. While the onion rings are hot, salt them to taste. Be sure the oil returns to 375°F before frying additional rings. Serve at once, or place the onion rings on an ovenproof dish, and keep them warm in a 200°F oven until ready to serve. ❧

STUFFED TOMATOES ON THE GRILL

6 large tomatoes
Ketchup to taste
1½ cups herb-
　　seasoned stuffing
½ cup Romano
　　cheese, grated
2 tablespoons
　　scallion, chopped
Dash pepper
2 tablespoons
　　melted butter

Preheat the grill to medium-high. Slice the top portion from each tomato; discard. Scoop out the pulp from each tomato. Chop and drain the pulp. Turn the tomato shells upside down on a paper towel to drain them.

In a bowl, combine the chopped tomato pulp, ketchup to taste, stuffing mix, cheese, green onion, pepper, and butter. Lightly salt the tomato shells; fill them with stuffing mixture. Wrap the bottom of each tomato in aluminum foil. Grill for about 30 minutes.

GRILLED RATATOUILLE

½ large red onion, quartered

1 package cherry tomatoes

2 zucchini, sliced

1 package sliced mushrooms

2 large yellow squash, sliced

1 red pepper, julienned

1 yellow pepper, julienned

1 green pepper, julienned

¾ cup balsamic vinegar

¼ cup Worcestershire

1 tablespoon olive oil

1 tablespoon Creole seasoning

1 teaspoon seasoned salt

Preheat the grill to medium. Mix all ingredients together in a large bowl. Place the mixture in a plastic storage bag. Marinate in the refrigerator for at least 2 hours. Preheat grill to medium-high. Grill the mixture in a grill wok or a basket until the vegetables are tender, stirring occasionally. The vegetables are best when somewhat charred. 🌿

7

VEGETABLES, SIDES & SALADS

EGGPLANT ROLL-UPS

1 medium eggplant, sliced lengthwise
  into ¼-inch-thick slices
Salt and pepper to taste
1 red pepper

1 green pepper
½ cup mayonnaise
1 tablespoon cranberry sauce
2 large pitas

Place the eggplant on a flat baking sheet; sprinkle both sides with salt and pepper. Let this stand 10 to 15 minutes.

Cut each pepper in half, and trim away the ribs and seeds. Cut an onion into rings. Preheat the grill to medium-high.

Place the eggplant, peppers, and onions on the grill, and cook 4 to 5 minutes for peppers and onions, 6 to 8 minutes for eggplant.

Grill the pitas for approximately 2 to 3 minutes until toasted; remove them from the grill.

Spread the cranberry sauce mixed with mayonnaise onto each pita; add the vegetables; and roll up pitas. 🐛

7

VEGETABLES, SIDES & SALADS

8 Desserts

(Left) Grilled Banana Split, page 267

GRILLED PEACHES WITH RASPBERRY PUREE

4 medium peaches, sliced in half and pitted
1 cup raspberries
¼ cup orange juice
¼ cup butter
2 tablespoons brown sugar
3 teaspoons honey
1 ounce rum

Preheat grill to medium. Combine butter, 1 teaspoon of honey, and brown sugar in a medium sauce pan. Bring to a low boil. Place the peaches in the sauce; let simmer 4 to 5 minutes.

Remove the peaches from the sauce; place on grill, cut side down. Turn peaches over when grill marks appear, about 2 to 3 minutes. Continue grilling 2 to 3 minutes more.

Remove peaches from the grill. In a blender, puree orange juice, raspberries, and remaining 2 teaspoons of honey to a sauce-like consistency. Place the peaches on a plate, and drizzle them with the raspberry mixture.

ADAM BYRD'S GRILLED BLACKBERRY COBBLER

2 tablespoons cornstarch

¼ cup cold water

1½ cups sugar

1 tablespoon lemon juice

4 cups blackberries, picked over, rinsed, and drained

1 cup flour

1 teaspoon baking powder

½ teaspoon salt

6 tablespoons cold butter, cut in small pieces

¼ cup boiling water

In a large bowl, stir together the cornstarch and ¼ cup cold water until the cornstarch is completely dissolved. Add 1 cup sugar, lemon juice, and blackberries; combine gently. Transfer the mixture to an 8-inch cast-iron skillet.

In a bowl, combine the flour, remaining sugar, baking powder, and salt. Blend in the butter until mixture resembles coarse meal. Add ¼ cup boiling water, and stir the mixture until it just forms dough.

Light the outer two burners of a three-burner grill to maximum heat. (I used the infrared burner and the right-hand burner on a Char-Broil Quantum.) Preheat until the temperature gauge on the lid reads 400°F. Light the side burner to medium-high heat; place skillet over this side. Bring the blackberry mixture to a boil, stirring constantly. Drop spoonfuls of dough carefully into the bubbling mixture. Transfer the cobbler to the center of the grill, and close the lid. Bake for 20 minutes or until the topping is golden. Serve warm. 🌿

"In my opinion, the blackberry syrup that accumulates is the best part of this dessert," says *"Men in Aprons"* writer Adam Byrd. He used handpicked black-berries from Sweet Berry Farm in Lexington, Texas, for this recipe.

BANANA BLISS

2 ripe bananas, unpeeled
2 cups miniature marshmallows
2 cups semisweet chocolate chips
Brown sugar
Aluminum foil

Leaving the peel on, slit the bananas lengthwise, but not all the way through the peel. Put half of the marshmallows and chocolate chips in the slit of each banana. Lightly sprinkle brown sugar on top of each banana. Wrap each banana tightly in foil, making sure to seal ends. Place on a medium-hot grill, seam side up, for about 7 minutes. Carefully remove bananas from grill; place in serving dish; unwrap; and serve hot. 👋

MISSISSIPPI RIVER PIE

1½ cups chocolate sandwich cookies, crumbled

2 tablespoons unsalted butter, melted

1½ quarts coffee ice cream

1 cup chunky-style peanut butter

8 ounces semisweet chocolate chips

2 cups heavy cream

1½ tablespoons confectioners' sugar

Preheat the oven to 350°F. Combine the crumbled cookies together with the melted butter in a medium bowl. Press the crumb mixture over the bottom of a 10-inch springform pan. Bake for about 14 to 16 minutes or until firm. Chill the crust in the freezer for about 15 minutes.

Place the ice cream in a large bowl, and allow it to soften slightly. Stir in the peanut butter; then press the mixture into the chilled crust. Quickly return the ice cream to the freezer for about 2 hours.

Just before serving, remove ice cream from the freezer. Next, make the chocolate sauce by slowly melting the chocolate chips and ½ cup of cream in a microwave or over a double boiler. Whip the remaining 1½ cups of cream until soft peaks form. Sprinkle the cream with sugar, and continue whipping until stiff peaks form. Release the pie from the springform pan, and cut it into wedges. To serve, pour warm chocolate sauce over each wedge, and top with whipped cream. 🍸

GRILLED PINEAPPLE POUND CAKE WITH PINEAPPLES, PEACHES & APPLES

POUND CAKE

1¾ cup cake flour

¾ teaspoon baking powder

¼ teaspoon salt

7 ounces butter
   (14 tablespoons)

⅞ cup sugar

3 eggs

3 tablespoons milk

1½ teaspoons dark rum

¾ cup fresh pineapple, diced

Preheat oven to 350°F. Butter and flour an 8 x 4 x 2½-inch loaf pan. In a large bowl, combine flour, baking powder, and salt; and set aside. With an electric mixer, cream butter and sugar until fluffy and pale in color. Beat in eggs one at a time, making sure each egg is absorbed before adding the next. Beat in half the flour mixture until just combined on low speed. Beat in the milk and rum. Add remaining flour mixture until just combined. Fold in pineapple.

Scrape the batter into the prepared pan. Smooth surface with a spatula. Bake approximately 60 minutes or until a wooden toothpick inserted in the center comes out clean. Let cake cool for about 10 minutes, and unmold. Note: your favorite store-bought pound cake is an acceptable substitute.

8 Servings • POUND CAKE—Prep: 25 min. • Bake: 1 hr. • Grill: 3 min.
• FRUIT—Prep: 10 min. • Grill: 10 min.

263

FRUIT

1 baking apple, such as Fuji, cored and cut into 12 slices

2 tablespoons maple syrup

1 teaspoon dark rum

1 tablespoon butter

Pinch of salt

Pinch of pepper

¼ teaspoon ground cinnamon

2 peaches, pitted, each cut into eighths

1 small pineapple, cleaned, cored and cut into 16 slices

¼ cup toasted almonds or hazelnuts, sliced

This delicious dessert was created by Char-Broil Guest Chef Gadi Weinrich. —CB

Preheat the grill to 400°F. Mix the apple slices with the maple syrup, rum, butter, salt, pepper, and cinnamon. Wrap the mixture up with aluminum foil, leaving room for air to circulate, and taking care not to puncture the foil so that the juices leak out. Grill for about 10 minutes. The apples should be tender, but not mushy.

While the apple is cooking, brush the grill grate with olive oil, and grill the peaches and pineapple. Mix fruit together in a mixing bowl.

Slice the pound cake into ¾-inch-thick slices. Place slices on top of buttered 4 x 5 sheets of aluminum foil. Grill for about 3 minutes until warmed and lightly toasted. Place the pound cake on a plate or serving platter, and arrange the fruit on top of the cake. Finish with ice cream, more fruit juices, fresh raspberries, whipped cream, and toasted almonds. 👉

GRILLED POUND CAKE WITH CHERRY-NUT ICE CREAM

¾ cup dried cherries

1 cup boiling water

5 tablespoons brandy

1½ pints vanilla ice cream, softened slightly

4 tablespoons semisweet chocolate, coarsely chopped

⅓ cup nuts (pecans, walnuts, or almonds), coarsely chopped

1 loaf pound cake

¼ cup unsalted butter

Place the cherries in a medium bowl. Pour 1 cup of boiling water over them. Let them stand until softened, about 10 minutes. Drain and pat them dry. Mix the cherries and 1 tablespoon of brandy in a small bowl. Place the ice cream in a large bowl. Mix in the cherries, chocolate, and nuts. Cover the ice cream mixture; freeze until firm, about 2 hours.

Preheat the grill to medium heat. Cut the pound cake into ½-inch slices. Brush both sides of each slice with melted butter. Grill the slices until lightly toasted, about 30 seconds per side.

Place two cake slices on each of eight dessert plates. Place a scoop of ice cream on top. Drizzle 1½ teaspoons of brandy over each serving. 🐝

WHOOPIE PIES

2 cups flour

1 cup sugar

5 tablespoons baking cocoa

1½ teaspoons baking soda

1 cup milk

1 egg, beaten

5 tablespoons margarine, softened

½ cup butter, softened

½ cup shortening

1 cup marshmallow crème

1 teaspoon vanilla extract

1 cup confectioners' sugar

Combine the flour, sugar, baking cocoa, and baking soda in a bowl; mix well. Add the milk, egg, and margarine, beating until blended. Drop 1 teaspoonful of the batter at a time onto an ungreased cookie sheet. Bake at 350°F for 10 to 15 minutes, or until the edges are crisp. Remove, and place on a wire rack to cool.

Beat the butter, shortening, and marshmallow crème in a mixer bowl until creamy. Add the vanilla, beating until blended. Add the confectioners' sugar. Beat for 2 minutes, scraping the bowl occasionally. Spread over half of the cookies, and top those with the remaining cookies. ✤

8

DESSERTS

GRILLED PINEAPPLE WITH YOGURT & WALNUTS

½ cup orange juice

½ cup mango juice or other fruit nectar

2 tablespoons maple syrup

1 tablespoon cornstarch

4 slices fresh pineapple, about ¾-inch-thick

1 cup of walnuts, chopped

1 cup of vanilla or other flavored yogurt

Oil for grilling

Preheat grill to medium low. Combine first four ingredients in a saucepan and bring to a boil; continue cooking for 3 to 5 minutes until sauce thickens. Brush pineapple slices with oil, and grill for 6 to 8 minutes, turning once. Remove pineapple from grill, and place in bowls. Top pineapple with yogurt, and sprinkle with walnuts. Serve immediately. 👆

GRILLED BANANA SPLITS

2 tablespoons melted butter

6 large ripe bananas

18 large scoops of your favorite ice cream

Chocolate sauce, as desired

Whipped cream, as desired

Chopped toasted nuts, as desired

6 maraschino cherries

Preheat the grill to medium. Melt the butter in a saucepan. Slice the bananas, still in their peels, lengthwise. Place the bananas cut side down onto the grates; grill for 3 to 4 minutes. Flip the bananas to the other side (peel side down). Brush the cut surfaces with melted butter, and grill for 2 to 3 additional minutes until the bananas are soft and lightly brown.

Remove the bananas from the grill, and let them cool. Remove the bananas from peels, and cut them into 1-inch chunks. Divide the cut bananas evenly among six serving dishes, and top each with three scoops of ice cream. Top each with chocolate sauce, whipped cream, nuts, and a cherry.

Tip: Let your guests customize their own banana splits. Set up a banana split bar with a variety of sauces and toppings. 🍌

GRILLED S'MORES

**8 graham crackers, each one
  split in half to make 16 pieces**
8 chocolate squares
16 large marshmallows
Skewers

Preheat the grill to high. If using wooden skewers, soak them in water before using them on the grill. Place the graham cracker halves on a warming tray. Set a square of chocolate on top of half of the crackers. Thread the marshmallows onto the end of each skewer. Hold the marshmallows just above the grill grate directly over high heat, turning slowly until lightly browned, about 2 to 3 minutes. Meanwhile, warm the graham crackers and chocolate over indirect heat. Place two roasted marshmallows on top of the melted chocolate, and gently press down with the top half of graham cracker. Serve immediately. 👆

WOOD-FIRED APPLE PECAN PIE

CRUST

1½ cups flour
¾ teaspoon salt
1½ tablespoons sugar
½ cup shortening
½ tablespoon butter
5 tablespoons water

FILLING

4 Granny Smith apples
3 Gala apples
2 cups pecans
1 cup brown sugar
1 tablespoon cinnamon
¾ cup flour

CRUMB TOPPING

1 cup flour
1 cup sugar
3 teaspoons cinnamon
½ cup (1 stick)
  butter, softened

For the crust, mix the flour, salt, and sugar. Cut in the shortening and butter. Mix in the water 1 tablespoon at a time using a fork. Roll out the dough, and shape it into a pie plate. Set this aside.

For the filling, peel, core, and slice the apples; then mix them with the other filling ingredients. Place the mixture in the crust, creating a mound in the middle.

For the crumb top, mix the flour, sugar, and cinnamon in a bowl. Cut in the butter until the mixture forms pea-size crumbs. Cover the apples with the crumb topping. Bake the pie in a smoker at 375°F for 40 to 45 minutes or until golden brown. 🖐

ADAM BYRD'S GRILLED PINEAPPLE SPEARS WITH BROWN-SUGAR GLAZE

½ pineapple, cut into long spears
1 tablespoon butter
½ cup brown sugar
1 teaspoon cinnamon
1 teaspoon fresh lemon juice

Preheat the grill to medium. Sprinkle the pineapple spears with half of the cinnamon and one teaspoon of brown sugar. (This will help to caramelize the pineapple when it hits the grill.)

In a small saucepan, heat the butter, brown sugar, lemon juice, and remaining cinnamon. Heat until mixture is bubbly and sugar is melted.

Grill the pineapple spears over direct heat for about 2 to 3 minutes per side, turning occasionally. Each time you turn, baste the pineapple with a brush of glaze. When finished, put pineapple spears on a platter, and drizzle the final amount of glaze on top. 🍴

Adam publishes a Web site called "Men in Aprons," dedicated to all things cooking-related. "Good desserts do not have to be complex cakes, cookies, or candies," he claims. "This particular pineapple was peeled and cored right in front of us in the grocery store, so we knew it would provide the ultimate in fresh flavor."

TIM BARR'S SMOKED PEARS WITH BERRY COMPOTE

4 ripe pears

Berry compote

1 cup white chocolate, melted

1 cup hazelnuts, toasted

BERRY COMPOTE

¼ cup pomegranate, blackberry, or apple juice

4 cups mixed berries, such as raspberries, blackberries, and blueberries, fresh or frozen

⅓ to ½ cup of turbinado sugar

¼ cup honey

½ teaspoon ground cloves

½ teaspoon ground nutmeg

1½ teaspoons vanilla extract

Place the juice in a medium saucepan over medium-low heat. Add the berries, and let them slowly break down for 30 to 40 minutes. (Allow frozen berries to thaw completely, and drain them well before cooking.) Do not let berries boil. When berries have cooked down, add the sugar, honey, cloves, and nutmeg; and continue cooking for another 30 to 40 minutes over low to medium heat, barely simmering, until the mixture is thick. Take the pan off the heat, and add the vanilla. Stir well, and allow the mixture to cool for at least an hour, preferably until it reaches room temperature, before putting it in the refrigerator overnight to set.

The next day, preheat the grill to medium. Halve the pears and spoon out the center to make a bowl out of each pear. Add compote to each. Save the remaining compote to use as wanted. Cook the pears in a foil pan or on a piece of foil in the smoker or grill at medium heat for 20 to 30 minutes, just until the pears start to soften. In the meantime, chop and toast the hazelnuts, and also melt the chocolate over the double boiler or carefully in microwave. Once the pears are done, spoon the chocolate over the compote and pears; top them with toasted hazelnuts; and serve warm. 🌶

Although his position with the U.S. Coast Guard takes him all over the country, Tim Barr still finds time to concoct great recipes like this for the grill. —CB

RICE PUDDING WITH DARK CHOCOLATE SAUCE

5 ounces uncooked
  white rice
2 pints milk
7 tablespoons
  butter
½ teaspoon vanilla
  extract
⅓ cup sugar
5 ounces dark
  chocolate chips
2 tablespoons water
1 tablespoon butter

In a medium saucepan, combine the rice, milk, butter, vanilla, nutmeg, and sugar. Bring the mixture to a gentle simmer over medium-high heat. Reduce the heat to low; cover; and simmer until the mixture is thick and pudding-like, about 10 minutes. Be careful not to scorch the bottom.

In a separate saucepan, heat the chocolate, water, and butter over low heat, and stir until the mixture is smooth and shiny, about 5 minutes. Add 2 to 3 heaping spoonfuls of chocolate sauce to each bowl, and stir. 🥄

[*This dessert is courtesy of Adam Byrd, who says, "This is the most decadent thing I have made to date."*]

9 Marinades, Sauces & Rubs

(Left) CB's Basic "Wet" Rub, page 282

ADOBO MARINADE

Yield: 1 cup
Prep: 5–10 min.
Marinate: 2 hr.–overnight
Use with: pork, chicken, fish

½ cup fresh orange juice
2 tablespoons lime juice
2 tablespoons wine vinegar
3 canned chipotle chilis
3 garlic cloves
2 teaspoons oregano
½ teaspoon black pepper
½ teaspoon salt
½ teaspoon ground cumin

In the bowl of a food processor, place all ingredients; puree. Makes enough marinade for six to eight pork chops. Place pork in self-sealing plastic bag; add marinade.

Adobo means seasoning or marinade in Spanish. This dark red marinade is often used in Filipino and Puerto Rican cooking. —CB

ASIAN MARINADE

Yield: ½ cup
Prep: 5–10 min.
Marinate: 1 hr.–overnight
Use with: pork chops, steak, chicken thighs, shrimp

¼ cup green onions, chopped
¼ cup hoisin sauce
1 tablespoon fresh ginger, minced

Combine ingredients well; then pour marinade over meat, poultry, or seafood. Marinate in a plastic ziplock bag or covered dish in the refrigerator.

CHIPOTLE MARINADE

Yield: ½ cup
Prep: 5–10 min.
Marinate: 2 hr.–overnight
Use with: steak, pork, chicken, seafood

⅓ cup fresh lime juice
¼ cup fresh cilantro, chopped
1 tablespoon brown sugar, packed
2 teaspoons chipotle chilies in adobo sauce, minced
2 tablespoons adobo sauce (from chilies)
2 cloves garlic, minced

Combine ingredients well; then pour marinade over meat, poultry, or seafood. Marinate in a plastic ziplock bag or covered dish in the refrigerator.

This Southwestern marinade is great for flank steak or pork tenderloin. —CB

GEORGE JV'S SECRET BEEF JERKY MARINADE

Yield: 1 cup
Prep: 5–10 min.
Marinate: 6 hr.–overnight
Use with: beef ribs, brisket, steak

½ cup soy sauce
1 clove garlic, mashed
2 tablespoons brown sugar
2 tablespoons ketchup
½ cup Worcestershire sauce
1¼ teaspoon salt
½ teaspoon onion powder
½ teaspoon pepper

Marinate in plastic bag or container for at least 6 hours or overnight.

George JV is a "Sizzle On the Grill" reader and frequent recipe contributor. —CB

QUICK CHIMICHURRI MARINADE

Yield: 1½ cups
Prep: 5–10 min.
Marinate: 2 hr.–overnight
Use with: London broil, flank steak, filet mignon

¾ cup prepared, non-creamy Caesar dressing
½ cup fresh parsley, chopped
¾ teaspoon crushed red pepper
Salt and pepper

Combine ingredients well; then pour marinade over meat. Marinate in a plastic ziplock bag or covered dish in the refrigerator.

Chimichurri originated in Argentina where it is a popular accompaniment to all types of grilled meats, especially steak. —CB

CB'S BASIC BRINE RECIPE

Yield: 4 cups brine
Prep time: 10 min.
Brining Time: 4 hr.–overnight
Use for: smoked turkey, chicken, beef brisket, salmon

¼ cup kosher salt
¼ cup packed brown sugar
4 cups hot water

In a medium bowl, combine the salt, sugar, and water. Whisk vigorously until salt and sugar have dissolved. Allow the mixture to cool. Pour brine over meat, poultry, or fish. Marinate for several hours or overnight in the refrigerator. Before smoking, rinse the meat's surface, and pat it dry.

Note: the meat should be fully submerged in the brine; make more brine by converting the recipe as needed.

CB'S BASIC DRY RUB

Yield: 1 cup
Prep: 10 min.
Marinate: 1 hr.–overnight
Use with: steak, roasts, ribs, chicken, turkey

½ cup garlic powder
⅛ cup kosher salt
⅛ cup powdered ginger
⅛ cup dry mustard

3 tablespoon coarse ground black pepper
1 tablespoon cumin powder
½ tablespoon curry powder

Combine ingredients in a bowl; mix thoroughly with a wire whisk. Pour the rub mixture into a clean, dry jar and tightly seal. Massage 2 to 3 tablespoons of the rub into the meat. Store the remaining rub away from light and heat.

CB'S INDIAN SPICE RUB

Yield: ½ cup
Prep: 10 min.
Use with: chicken, fish, pork, vegetables

1 tablespoon cumin seeds
1 tablespoon coriander seeds
1 tablespoon fennel seeds
1 tablespoon kosher salt
½ tablespoon curry powder
¼ to ½ teaspoon cayenne pepper

4 large cloves garlic
¼ cup fresh lemon juice
½ tablespoon vegetable oil

In a small, heavy skillet, toast cumin, coriander, and fennel seeds over high heat, stirring until fragrant and lightly browned (about 2 minutes). Cool on a plate. Place seeds in blender, and whirl until finely ground. Add salt, curry powder, cayenne, and garlic; blend to a paste. Add lemon juice and oil; blend to combine.

CB'S DRY SUGAR RUB

Yield: ¼ cup
Prep: 10 min.
Use with: smoked beef, pork, chicken, turkey

2 tablespoons sugar
1 tablespoon chili powder
1 teaspoon black pepper
½ tablespoon ground cumin
½ tablespoon paprika

½ tablespoon salt
¼ teaspoon dry mustard
Dash of cinnamon

Combine ingredients in a bowl; mix thoroughly with a wire whisk. Pour the rub mixture into a clean, dry jar, and tightly seal. Massage 2 to 3 tablespoons of the rub into the meat. Store the remaining rub away from light and heat.

CB'S SOUTHWEST-STYLE RUB

Yield: 1 cup
Prep: 10 min.
Marinate: 20 min.
Use with: pork, chicken, beef

DRY INGREDIENTS

¼ cup chili powder
¼ cup packed brown sugar
⅛ cup ground cumin
⅛ cup kosher salt
⅛ cup black pepper
1 teaspoon ground cinnamon

WET INGREDIENTS

1 tablespoon Worcestershire sauce
⅛ cup apple cider vinegar
1 tablespoon fresh garlic, minced (or 1 tablespoon garlic powder)
1 teaspoon hot sauce

Mix the dry ingredients; add the wet ingredients; mix again. Store mixture in the refrigerator for up to 3 days. Apply the rub to meat; let meat rest for about 20 minutes before slow cooking. Note: use plastic gloves or plastic sandwich bags over your hands to prevent irritation from the spices.

I developed this rub to please guests who enjoy something a little spicy on their ribs or other slow-cooked meat. I think it works well with just about any meat, but particularly with pork and chicken when rubbed on about 20 minutes or so before you start the slow-cooking process. If you like "dry" ribs, I think another dose can also go on after grilling (or toward the end) to add extra "oomph!"—CB

CB'S BASIC "WET" RUB

Yield: ½ cup
Prep: 10 min.
Marinate: 20 min.
Use with: pork, chicken, beef, seafood, vegetables

1 tablespoon garlic, minced
¼ cup brown sugar
⅛ teaspoon coarse salt
⅛ teaspoon fresh ground black pepper
1 tablespoon Worcestershire sauce
⅛ cup balsamic vinegar

Combine dry ingredients; add wet ingredients; mix again. Apply to meat about 20 minutes before slow cooking. Note: use plastic gloves or plastic sandwich bags over your hands to prevent irritation from the spices. Wet rub may be stored in the refrigerator for up to 3 days.

This rub forms a paste when the wet and dry ingredients are mixed together.—CB

CB'S TERIYAKI-STYLE SAUCE

Yield: ¾ cup
Prep: 5–10 min.
Use with: steak, pork, chicken, shrimp, vegetables

½ cup dark brown sugar, firmly packed
½ cup soy sauce
¼ cup of hot water (or more to taste)
1 tablespoon Asian sesame oil
1 teaspoon dry Chinese-style mustard
1 teaspoon ground ginger
1 teaspoon orange zest

Combine the ingredients in saucepan. Heat, and brush on meat during final minutes of grilling.

Teryaki sauce is a great finishing touch for almost any grilled food, especially steak, chicken, pork—even vegetables. —CB

CB'S BASIC BEER SAUCE

Yield: 3 cups
Prep: 15 min.
Use with: smoked beef brisket, pork butt, ribs

1 12-ounce can or bottle of ale or dark beer
½ cup apple cider
½ cup water
¼ cup peanut oil
2 medium shallots, chopped
3 garlic cloves, chopped
1 tablespoon Worcestershire sauce
1 teaspoon hot sauce

Combine the ingredients in a saucepan. Heat the mixture, and brush it on the meat during the final minutes of grilling.

Beer seems to be plentiful around many backyard barbecues. Try using a richer beer to make this excellent "mop" for your low- and slow-cooking barbecue or grilled meats. —CB

NORTH CAROLINA BBQ SAUCE I

Yield: 2 cups
Prep: 15 min.
Marinate: 2 hr.
Use with: smoked and barbecued beef brisket, pork butt, ribs, chicken

2 cups cider vinegar
¼ cup brown sugar

1 tablespoon crushed red pepper
3 teaspoons salt
1½ teaspoons ground cayenne chili
1 teaspoon freshly ground black pepper
1 teaspoon ground white pepper

Combine all ingredients in a large bowl; mix well; and let stand for 2 hours to blend the flavors.

NORTH CAROLINA BBQ SAUCE II

Yield: 2 cups

Prep: 15 min.

Use with: smoked and barbecued beef brisket, pork butt, ribs, chicken

2 cups cider vinegar

¼ cup brown sugar

1 tablespoon crushed red pepper

3 teaspoons salt

1½ teaspoons ground cayenne chili

1 teaspoon freshly ground black pepper

1 teaspoon ground white pepper

1 cup ketchup

1 teaspoon Worcestershire sauce

½ teaspoon cinnamon

Combine all ingredients in a large bowl; mix well; and let stand for 2 hours to blend the flavors.

MEMPHIS BBQ SAUCE

Yield: 3 cups

Prep: 15 min.

Cook: 25 min.

Use with: pork ribs, beef ribs, chicken, brisket, pork butt

¼ cup apple cider vinegar

½ cup prepared mustard

2 cups ketchup

3 tablespoons Worcestershire sauce

1 tablespoon black pepper, finely ground

¼ cup brown sugar

2 teaspoons celery salt

2 tablespoons chili powder

1 tablespoon onion powder

2 teaspoons garlic powder

¼ to ½ teaspoon cayenne pepper (optional)

2 teaspoons liquid smoke (optional)

2 tablespoons canola oil

Combine all ingredients, except the oil, in a saucepan. Bring them to a boil, stirring to dissolve the sugar. Reduce the heat, and simmer for 25 minutes, stirring occasionally. With a whisk, blend in the oil until incorporated.

TEXAS BBQ SAUCE

Yield: 3 cups (enough for 6 pounds of meat)

Prep: 15 min.

Cook: 20 min.

Use with: poultry, pork, beef ribs

1 tablespoon salt

1 teaspoon barbecue seasoning mix

½ teaspoon pepper

3 tablespoons brown sugar

¼ cup ketchup

½ cup Worcestershire sauce

3 tablespoons Dijon mustard

1 tablespoon liquid smoke

1 cup brewed, strong coffee

½ cup vinegar

1 cup olive oil

Mix the ingredients in the order given, using a hand-held mixer when adding the oil. Simmer slowly until thickened. Keep hot. Use to baste poultry, pork, or beef ribs.

SOUTH CAROLINA RED BBQ SAUCE

Yield: 2 cups
Prep: 20 min.
Use with: ribs, steak, chicken

1½ cups apple cider vinegar
½ cup ketchup
1 tablespoon brown sugar
1 teaspoon salt
½ teaspoon crushed red pepper

Combine all the ingredients; stir until sugar and salt dissolve. Taste, and adjust the sauce by adding more ketchup and brown sugar to reduce the tangy flavor. Sauce can be prepared up to 3 days ahead; covered; and refrigerated.

CB'S EZ DR. PEPPER BBQ SAUCE

Yield: 3 cups
Prep: 10 min.
Cook: 10 min.
Use with: ribs, chicken, pork

12 ounces regular Dr. Pepper
1 cup tomato ketchup
¼ cup apple cider vinegar
¼ cup Worcestershire Sauce
⅛ teaspoon hot pepper sauce
2 tablespoon CB's Basic Dry Rub (See page 280.)
2 teaspoons paprika

Combine Dr. Pepper, ketchup, vinegar, Worcestershire, and hot pepper sauce in a saucepan on your grill's side burner; bring mixture to just below a boil. Stirring gently, mix in the dry ingredients. Bring to a boil. Brush the mixture on during grilling, or serve as a dipping sauce.

Hot Dr. Pepper is served at the soft-drink company's headquarters during the winter months. I like to drink the cold variety when I grill, and I started adding it to some homemade sauces a few years ago. Use this as a mop sauce, glaze, or dipping sauce for ribs, chicken, and all manner of pork!—CB

REVEREND STEPHEN'S TEMPTATION BBQ SAUCE

Yield: 3½ cups
Prep: 15 min.
Cook: 20 min.
Use with: smoked or barbecued ribs, brisket, chicken

This recipe was sent to CB by a BBQ fan known as Reverend Stephen.

½ onion, minced
4 cloves garlic, minced
¾ cup bourbon
½ teaspoon ground black pepper
½ tablespoon salt
2 cups ketchup
¼ cup tomato paste
⅓ cup apple cider vinegar
2 tablespoons liquid smoke
¼ cup Worcestershire sauce
¼ cup packed brown sugar
½ teaspoon hot pepper sauce (or to taste)

In a large skillet over medium heat, combine the onion, garlic, and bourbon. Simmer for 10 minutes or until the onion is translucent. Mix in the ground black pepper, salt, ketchup, tomato paste, vinegar, liquid smoke, Worcestershire sauce, brown sugar, and hot pepper sauce. Bring this to a boil. Reduce the heat to medium-low, and simmer for 20 minutes. If you prefer a smoother sauce, pour the mixture through a strainer.

9

MARINADES, SAUCES & RUBS

CB'S GEORGIA-STYLE MUSTARD SAUCE

Yield: 2½ cups
Prep: 10 min.
Cook: 20–30 min.
Use with: pork, chicken

2 tablespoons vegetable oil
½ cup Vidalia or other sweet onion, minced
1 cup prepared mustard
½ cup fresh lemon juice (or lemonade)
¼ cup dark brown sugar, firmly packed
¼ cup apple cider vinegar

1 teaspoon celery seed
1 teaspoon kosher salt
1 teaspoon powdered ginger

Heat the oil in a medium-size, nonreactive saucepan over medium heat. Add the onions, and sauté until translucent, about 3 to 4 minutes. Add the rest of the ingredients; blend well. Bring the mixture to a boil; then reduce the heat and simmer for 15 to 20 minutes, stirring occasionally.

CB'S LEMON-GARLIC BUTTER SAUCE

Yield: ¼ cup per serving
Prep: 15 min.
Cook: 5 min.
Use with: fish fillets, shrimp, lobster, chicken, steak, vegetables

PER SERVING

2 tablespoons clarified butter (See note.)
½ fresh lemon, juiced
2 tablespoons light olive oil or canola oil
1 clove garlic, crushed
¼ teaspoon lemon zest

Combine the ingredients in a saucepan. Heat the mixture, and brush it on food during the final minutes of grilling and on the serving plate.

Clarified butter has a higher smoke point than regular butter. Place 1 pound of unsalted butter in a saucepan at the back of the stove; cover; and allow the butter to melt while you're cooking. Skim off the solids that have risen to the surface. Use immediately, or pour into a glass container to freeze. —CB

CB'S TARRAGON-BUTTER SAUCE

Yield: ¼ cup per serving
Prep: 10 min.
Use with: seafood, chicken, vegetables

PER SERVING

2 tablespoons clarified butter (See note above.)
2 tablespoons light olive oil or canola oil
1 tablespoon fresh tarragon, chopped

Combine all ingredients in a saucepan. Heat the mixture, and brush it on food during the final minutes of grilling. May also be used as a dipping sauce, especially for grilled shrimp, crab legs, or lobster.

This is an excellent flavor to add to grilled fish such as tilapia or salmon. —CB

ROASTED GARLIC

Yield: about ¼ cup
Prep: 5–10 min.
Cook: 30–40 min. on the grill, 35–45 min. in
  the oven
Use with: steak, chicken, pork, grilled corn, or
  as a spread on grilled bruschetta

1 whole garlic bulb
1 teaspoon canola oil
1 small rosemary sprig (optional)
Freshly ground black pepper to taste
Salt to taste (optional)

Cut ½ inch off the top of the garlic bulb so that individual cloves are exposed. Cut an 8-inch-square sheet of heavy-duty aluminum foil. Place the garlic bulb on the foil; add oil to the cut end of the garlic bulb. Place the herb sprig across the bulb, and season with pepper and salt. Wrap foil around the bulb.

Preheat the grill to high. When ready, place the wrapped bulb on the grill and cook for 30 to 40 minutes, turning carefully several times.

Remove the bulb from the grill; let cool. Squeeze the cooked garlic bulb by hand, and the delicious, soft pulp will come forth. If desired, the garlic can be roasted in the oven at 375°F for 45 minutes to 1 hour until soft.

ROASTED-GARLIC MAYO

Yield: 1 cup
Prep: 20 min.
Use with: fish, chicken, vegetables

2 whole heads garlic, roasted (See recipe above.)
1 cup prepared mayonnaise
½ teaspoon lemon juice

Squeeze garlic pulp from cloves into the work bowl of a food processor; pulse three or four times until smooth. Add the mayonnaise and lemon juice, and blend until smooth and well combined. Use this mayonnaise immediately, or cover and refrigerate for up to 2 days.

BETTER-THAN-HOMEMADE MAYO

Yield: 1 cup
Prep: 20 min.
Use with: fish, chicken, pork

1 cup prepared mayonnaise
1½ tablespoons olive oil
¼ teaspoon fresh lemon juice
¼ teaspoon garlic, minced
Tabasco sauce to taste

Whisk the ingredients together. This mayonnaise can be used immediately, or covered and refrigerated for 2 to 3 weeks.

ROASTED RED PEPPER MAYO

Yield: 1¼ cups

Prep: 20 min.

Use with: seafood, chicken, vegetables

2 red peppers, roasted and chopped

1 clove garlic, chopped

1 cup prepared mayonnaise

¼ teaspoon cayenne pepper

Combine the peppers and garlic in a food processor; blend until smooth. Add the mayonnaise and cayenne until combined. Use this mayonnaise immediately, or cover and refrigerate for up to 2 days.

CB'S ORANGE AIOLI

Yield: 1¼ cups
Prep: 10 min.
Use with: seafood, chicken, vegetables

1 cup mayonnaise
¼ cup orange juice
1 tablespoon hot pepper sauce
½ teaspoon sugar
½ teaspoon garlic, chopped
½ teaspoon prepared horseradish
2 tablespoons scallions, chopped

Stir all ingredients together and refrigerate until ready to use. Because it only keeps for a few days, make just enough to use in about 24 hours.

Aioli is a word that has been popping up on restaurant menus all over the place. It's really just flavored mayonnaise. So whether you make your own mayo or purchase it in jars like most folks, experiment with some new flavors and impress your friends when you call it aioli. (A-OH-LEE!)—CB

AVOCADO CREAM

Yield: 1½ cups
Prep: 30 min.
Use with: Garlic-Lime
Alaska Prawns
(See page 190.)

2 avocados, 1½ pounds total
½ cup sour cream
2 tablespoons mayonnaise
2 tablespoons lime juice
1 teaspoon ground dried ancho
chiles or chili powder
½ teaspoon salt

Peel ripe avocados; cut into chunks; and put in the work bowl of a food processor. Add sour cream, mayonnaise, lime juice, ancho chiles or chili powder, and salt; blend until smooth. Taste, and add more lime juice and salt if desired. Scrape into small bowl.

GUACAMOLE

Yield: about 2 cups

Prep: 15 min., plus 1 hr. refrigeration

Use with: Holy Guacamole Burgers (see page 60), taco chips, raw vegetables

3 to 4 large, ripe avocados

5 cloves roasted garlic (See page 290.)

Juice of 1 lime

2 tablespoons cilantro, chopped

½ teaspoon red pepper flakes

1 large tomato, diced

Salt and pepper to taste

Peel the avocados; discard the pits; and remove any bad spots. Cut them into ½-inch cubes. In a food processor, blend together the avocado, garlic, lime juice, cilantro, red pepper, and salt and pepper. Move to a serving dish. Stir in the chopped tomato. Cover, and refrigerate for 1 hour.

CLASSIC PARMESAN-BASIL PESTO

Yield: about 2 cups

Prep: 5–10 min.

Use with: pork tenderloin, pork chops, fish steaks, chicken breast, vegetables

1⅓ cups basil leaves

1½ teaspoons garlic, chopped

¼ cup pine nuts, toasted

½ cup Parmesan cheese, grated

¼ cup olive oil

Salt and pepper to taste

Combine first four ingredients in a food processor; pulse three or four times. With motor running, slowly drizzle in olive oil until mixture blends into a paste. Season with salt and pepper to taste.

SUN-DRIED TOMATO PESTO

Yield: about 2 cups

Prep: 5–10 min.

Use with: pork tenderloin, pork chops, fish steaks, chicken breast, vegetables

1½ cups sun-dried tomatoes, packed in oil, drained

6 garlic cloves, peeled

1 cup Parmesan cheese, grated

1 cup fresh basil leaves

½ cup olive oil

2 tablespoons balsamic vinegar

Combine all ingredients in a food processor or blender; blend until mixture is smooth and well combined.

HORSERADISH SAUCE

Yield: 1½ cups
Prep: 15 min.
Use with: smoked prime rib

1 3-ounce package cream cheese
1 cup sour cream
1 teaspoon onion, grated
2 tablespoons horseradish
¼ teaspoon sugar

¼ teaspoon salt
¼ teaspoon pepper

Combine all ingredients in a blender.

This is a perfect accompaniment to a smoked rib roast. (See page 88.)—CB

MAPLE-BOURBON GLAZE

Yield: 1 cup
Prep: 10 min.
Use with: chicken, turkey, pork, ribs

1 tablespoon vegetable oil
½ cup onion, chopped
½ cup pure maple or pancake syrup
½ cup ketchup
¼ cup bourbon or other whiskey
1 teaspoon hot pepper sauce (optional)
½ cup mayonnaise

In a medium saucepan, heat oil over medium-high heat. Cook onion, stirring occasionally, for 5 minutes or until golden.

Add the syrup, ketchup, bourbon, and hot pepper sauce to the saucepan. Bring to a boil over high heat. Reduce heat to low, and simmer, stirring occasionally, for 5 minutes or until sauce thickens slightly.

Remove the pan from the heat. Using a wire whisk, stir in mayonnaise until smooth.

SWEET ALE MUSTARD

Yield: 2 cups
Prep: 20 min.
Marinate: 1 hr.–overnight
Use with: brats, sausage, burgers

½ heaping cup mustard seeds
¼ cup dry mustard
½ cup malt vinegar
1 cup medium-bodied ale
3 tablespoons honey
2 teaspoons salt

¼ teaspoons cayenne pepper
¼ teaspoons paprika

Combine the mustard seeds and mustard with the vinegar, and cover. Allow the mixture to sit at room temperature for at least 1 hour or longer to mellow the strong flavors.

Combine the mustard mixture with the remaining ingredients in a food processor; blend to a coarse puree. Refrigerate mixture for at least 24 hours; then taste, and adjust the seasoning to your preference.

CB'S "WHAT'S IN THE KITCHEN CUPBOARD?" TACO SAUCE

Yield: ¾ cup

Prep: However long it takes to find stuff

Cook: However long it takes to put it together and taste-test to get it right

Use with: Just about everything

5 tablespoons ketchup

4 tablespoons creamy horseradish

1 tablespoon wasabi

1 tablespoon black bean garlic sauce

1 tablespoon garlic, minced

1 tablespoon hot sauce

Mix all ingredients together, and serve chilled.

> *This sauce was developed because I was out of regular salsa. I opened the fridge and the cupboard and put together some "tastes" from memory that I thought would work. I didn't tell anyone what was in it until they began telling me how great it tasted!* —CB

SPICY-SWEET HOMEMADE KETCHUP

Yield: 2 cups

Prep: 20 min.

Cook: 45–50 min.

Use with: steak, burgers, hot dogs, sausage

1 15-ounce can crushed tomatoes, liquid reserved

1 6-ounce can tomato paste

½ small onion, minced

½ red pepper, minced

½ cup water

¼ cup cider vinegar

3 tablespoons corn syrup

1 tablespoon brown sugar

1 teaspoon ground allspice

1 teaspoon salt

¾ teaspoon fresh-ground black pepper

¼ teaspoon ground cloves

¼ teaspoon cinnamon

Combine all ingredients in a nonreactive saucepan. Bring to a boil over high heat; reduce the heat to medium-low; and cook the mixture for 45 to 50 minutes, stirring occasionally at first and constantly at the end. This ketchup is the proper consistency when it is a bit thinner than store-bought versions. Can be refrigerated in a covered container for 2 to 3 weeks.

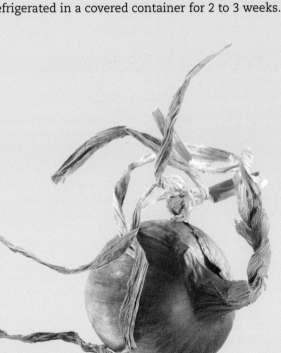

RESOURCES

This list of manufacturers and associations is meant to be a general guide to additional industry and product-related sources. It is not intended as a listing of products and manufacturers represented by the photographs in this book.

The Alaska Seafood Marketing Institute (ASMI)
888-800-2486
www.alaskaseafood.org
Alaska's official seafood marketing agency offers a consumer recipe database on its Web site.

Cattlemen's Beef Board and National Cattlemen's Beef Association
www.beefitswhatsfordinner.com
Offers tips, food safety information, and recipes for preparing beef through its Web site.

Char-Broil
866-239-6777
www.charbroil.com
Official Web site for the Char-Broil company.

Hearth, Patio & Barbecue Association (HPBA)
703-522-0086
www.hpba.org
International trade association that promotes manufacturers and retailers of hearth, patio, and barbecue products.

Kansas City Barbeque Society (KCBS)
800-963-5227
www.kcbs.us
The Kansas City Barbeque Society is the world's largest nonprofit organization dedicated to promoting and enjoying barbecue.

Men in Aprons
www.meninaprons.net
A Web site dedicated to all things cooking and grilling related.

National Pork Board
www.theotherwhitemeat.com
Offers tips, recipes, menu ideas, and information on safe food handling through its Web site.

National Turkey Federation
www.eatturkey.com
Develops consumer education and information for the public on turkey nutrition, seasonal and holiday recipes, and preparation basics.

Sizzle on the Grill
www.sizzleonthegrill.com
Char-Broil-sponsored newsletter and Web site featuring grilling tips and recipes.

United States Department of Agriculture (USDA) Food Safety and Inspection Service
www.fsis.usda.gov
The Web site offers consumer safety information on buying, storing, preparing, and cooking meat and poultry.

USDA Meat & Poultry Hotline
1-888-MPHotline
1-888-674-6854
Answers questions about safe storage, handling, and preparation of meat and poultry products.

GUIDE TO BASIC BEEF CUTS

TENDER STEAKS: Most of these come from the center (rib and loin sections) and are best cooked using dry-heat methods such as grilling.

Premium tender steaks include top loin (strip), T-Bone, Porterhouse, ribeye, rib, and tenderloin.

Family-priced tender steaks include shoulder center, top sirloin, top blade (flat iron), chuck eye and round tip.

LESS-TENDER STEAKS: These are primarily from the more muscled fore- and hindquarters and are better suited for moist-heat cooking. However, some less-tender cuts may be cooked with dry heat after being tenderized. Less tender steaks include full-cut round, top round, eye round and bottom round, chuck shoulder, chuck 7-bone, chuck arm, chuck blade, flank, and skirt.

CUBED STEAKS: These are mechanically tenderized steaks, usually from the round.

Courtesy of the Cattlemen's Beef Board and National Cattlemen's Beef Association

SAFE COOKING TEMPERATURES

Cook foods to the recommended safe minimum internal temperatures listed below.

Product	Type	Internal Temperature (°F)
BEEF & VEAL	Ground	160
	Steak and roasts medium	160
	Steak and roasts medium rare	145
CHICKEN & TURKEY	Breasts	165
	Ground, stuffing, and casseroles	165
	Whole bird, legs, thighs, and wings	165
EGGS	Any type	160
FISH & SHELLFISH	Any type	145
LAMB	Ground	160
	Steak and roasts medium	160
	Steaks and roasts medium rare	145
LEFTOVERS	Any type	165
PORK	Chops, fresh (raw) ham ground, ribs, and roasts	160
	Fully cooked ham (to reheat)	140

Courtesy: United States Dept. of Agriculture

INDEX

INDEX

INDEX

Have a home gardening, decorating, or improvement project?
Look for these and other fine **Creative Homeowner** books wherever books are sold

DESIGN IDEAS FOR DECKS & PATIOS
Features comprehensive information and inspiration for designing and building a deck or patio.

Over 350 photographs.
224 pp.
8½" × 10⅞"
$19.95 (US)
$23.95 (CAN)
BOOK #: 279534

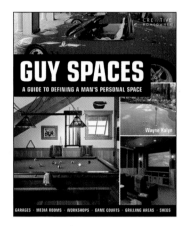

GUY SPACES
Offers ideas for enhancing workshops, garages, media rooms, gyms, and other man-friendly spaces in the home.

Over 250 photographs.
208 pp.
9¼" × 10⅞"
$19.95 (US)
$23.95 (CAN)
BOOK #: 279529

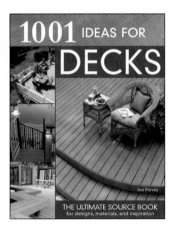

1001 IDEAS FOR DECKS
Covers design solutions, building techniques, and the latest information on deck materials.

Over 450 photographs and illustrations.
287 pp.
8½" × 10⅞"
$ 24.95 (US)
$ 29.95 (CAN)
BOOK #: 277194

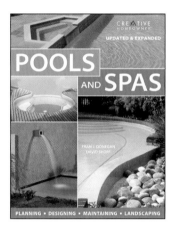

POOLS AND SPAS
Offers ideas and advice on the complete process of planning, building, and maintaining a pool/spa.

Over 300 photographs.
240 pp.
8½" × 10⅞"
$21.95 (US)
$25.95 (CAN)
BOOK #: 277860

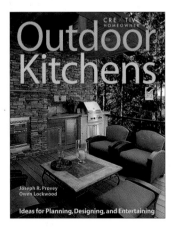

OUTDOOR KITCHENS
Includes planning and design advice and easy how-to projects from top designers.

Over 335 photographs.
224 pp.
8½" × 10⅞"
$21.95 (US)
$25.95 (CAN)
BOOK #: 277571

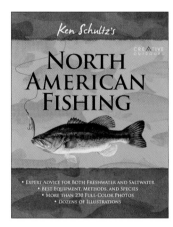

KEN SCHULTZ'S NORTH AMERICAN FISHING
Features all the techniques and equipment needed to become a successful angler.

Over 230 photographs and illustrations.
256 pp., 9" × 11"
$24.95 (US)
$27.95 (CAN)
BOOK #: 252083

For more information and to order direct, go to **www.creativehomeowner.com**